101 Creative Writing Activities for Aspiring Authors

Written by Tracey Ann Schofield

Illustrated by Alex Glikin

Teaching & Learning Company

1204 Buchanan St., P.O Box 10

Carthage, IL 62321-0010

This book belongs to

_____

Dedication

For my mom and dad:
my (beloved) parents,
my (biggest) fans,
my (best) friends.

I love you!

Tracey

Cover design by Peggy Larson

Table of Contents

Dear Teacher or Parent,

101 Creative Writing Activities for Aspiring Authors is a collection of unique writing activities designed to stimulate the interest and creativity of children and adults. Based on my personal/educator/parent/"If it's fun, kids will do it" philosophy, the activities in this book are both fun and functional. When we help children find pleasure in the writing process, we present them with an educational power tool. If they can have fun writing, they *will* write. And every time they put pencil to paper, they improve their writing skills.

The format of the book is straightforward. Each named and numbered writing activity has two features: a brief description and an example. I learned the hard way that children are more inclined to participate in a creative writing activity if they have a clear understanding of the desired outcome. When I first began facilitating creative writing in the classroom, I presented one of these very exercises—and watched, dismayed, as 35 pencils hovered in the air, unwilling or unable to commit to paper. In desperation, I read my own response, prepared in advance. The effect was magical. As soon as I had uttered my last syllable, the eyes before me scrunched in concentration, the heads bowed low over their papers and the pencils began to scribble furiously. The example of a finished product had stirred the dormant creative juices of those willing children, and they rewarded me unanimously with their enthusiasm and their effort.

The other important lesson that experience has taught me is that children love to share their work, and this is a critical component of my creative writing program. Children want their peers, their educators and their parents to hear what they have to say. They are proud of their thoughts and their ability to put them on paper. Shyness or embarrassment might make some children initially reluctant to read their writing out loud, but once they get going, they're like snowballs rolling downhill: continually gaining momentum and impossible to stop! Respectful of each child's right to privacy, I make it a point to leave enough time after a writing exercise to call upon every raised hand and encourage the sharing of all writing—even the silly stuff—that is not offensive or hurtful. It is the writing process, not the written product, that is important. And I abide by the principle that *any* writing is *good* writing.

One of the most wonderful features of this book is its infinite shelf life. Since our minds will produce different thoughts about a single subject on any given day—or during any given minute!—each writing activity can be done over and over again. The activities are arranged alphabetically but can be done and redone in any order, any number of times. Intended for use in the classroom and in the home, every activity is designed to provide children with a quick and enjoyable writing experience. Teachers can present an exercise during school hours or assign one as homework to be shared the next day; parents can serve up a short activity before dinner or bed.

One final note: I strongly encourage adults—teachers and parents—to play along, taking their own turn with the pencil and keeping their own *101 Creative Writing Activities for Aspiring Authors* notebook. By participating actively in the writing process, adults give credibility to writing practice. By sharing their thoughts, they encourage the kind of reciprocal communication that is the hallmark of every healthy professional and personal relationship.

I hope you and your children enjoy *101 Creative Writing Activities for Aspiring Authors* and have as much fun with the activities in this book as I did!

Sincerely,

Tracey

Tracey Ann Schofield

How to Use This Book

- The activities in this book are arranged alphabetically but can be done—and redone—in any order.

- Authors should use a three-ring binder and sheets of lined, loose-leaf paper for their writing. Only one activity should occupy each page, and only the front side of each page should be used. (This setup allows for easy organization of written material. Activities can be grouped according to their name and number, subject matter or style.)

- Children should be encouraged to keep and file all of their creative writing. There can be a kernel of brilliance in any raw thought, even one that is crude and poorly expressed. Saving rough material allows children the opportunity to salvage later: to edit, to rewrite or to extract that single bright kernel for use elsewhere.

- These writing activities should not be submitted for grading. Pressure to perform can inhibit a child's creativity. Instead, students could be marked on their participation and effort. It is, after all, the act of writing—not the written product—that is important here.

- Sentence structure, punctuation and the organization of thoughts are not the focus. These activities provide an opportunity for unfettered creative thinking and pure writing enjoyment. These goals should not be constrained or compromised by the enforcement of grammatical or stylistic rules.

- In the example that accompanies each writing activity, the author has written to the level of her own ability. All authors should be encouraged to do the same. The writing can be as simple or complex as the writer wishes it to be.

- Although a variety of subject suggestions for many of the activities is provided, some children may need additional prompting. Facilitators should offer ideas until a child's imagination is captured and writing flows easily.

- Facilitators should leave enough time after each writing activity to allow all participants an opportunity to share their work. The feedback loop is an important part of any creative writing program. The reading of written work reinforces the writing experience and helps to foster enthusiasm and enjoyment.

- Children should never be forced to read—or submit—what they have written. Sharing should be strictly voluntary. The right to privacy is paramount to the creative process. Some children will not write freely and openly if they believe that their thoughts, feelings and experiences will be exposed.

Activity 1

Absolutely NOT!

Write down one thing that you absolutely would not do for all of the money in the world. Explain your choice.

I absolutely would not, in a million years, for a million dollars . . .

    . . . live downtown in a major city center.

I hate crowds. I hate noise. I hate pollution. I hate confusion. I hate having neighbors within whispering distance.

I love the country. I love the sound of birds singing and trees whistling in the wind. I love space. I love privacy. I love tranquillity.

All the money in the world could not bring me joy if I was snatched from my country home and imprisoned in the city. With a broken heart and a broken spirit, I would live as a caged bird, pining for my freedom from behind bars.

Activity 2

Acrostic Personalities

An acrostic poem is written using the letters of a word to begin each line in the poem. Write an acrostic poem featuring one of your personality traits. Try to make each line relate in some way to the word you are using.

Charming

Charismatic
Humble
Appealing
Refreshing
Mesmerizing
Intriguing
Nonchalant
Genuine

All-Time Time Wasters

How do you "waste" your time? In other words, what things do you do that you don't have to do—and shouldn't do— when you really should be doing something else?

When I am procrastinating*, which is something I have elevated to an art form, I find an incredible number of ways to waste my precious time.

I. . . . go to the bathroom every few minutes

read books, magazines, flyers, soup labels— anything I can get my hands on

. . . clean up (which is something I normally despise!)

. . . do laundry

. . . talk on the phone

. . . daydream

. . . wander aimlessly around the house

. . . go shopping

. . . put myself to sleep

. . . think of a million reasons why I should put off what I should be doing!

*procrastinate: to put off taking action until a future time; to defer or postpone

America's Most Wanted

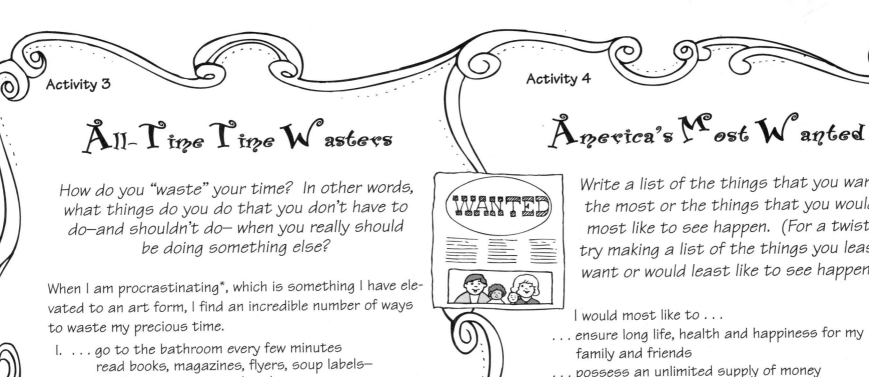

Write a list of the things that you want the most or the things that you would most like to see happen. (For a twist, try making a list of the things you least want or would least like to see happen.)

I would most like to . . .

. . . ensure long life, health and happiness for my family and friends

. . . possess an unlimited supply of money

. . . find a solution to the world's most pressing problems: overpopulation, resource depletion, species extinction, war, poverty, homelessness and hunger

. . . sleep in a king-sized bed

. . . surprise my husband with the car of his dreams

. . . hire a live-in maid

. . . travel the globe (or at least visit Disney World!)

. . . achieve my fullest potential as a human being, woman and mother

. . . freeze time now, while my kids are still young

Anything but This

What would you rather be doing right now?

I would rather be lying on a blanket on a hot, white sand beach with a good book and a cool drink, next to a large, roan gelded horse named Utah's Zion who is recovering in the shade of a beautiful green palm tree and is still wet from our recent exhilarating, bareback gallop through the clear blue water at the ocean's edge.

Backronyms

An **acronym** is a word formed by the combining of initial letters or syllables and letters of a series of words or a compound term. Some examples of well-known acronyms are IRS (Internal Revenue Service), FBI (Federal Bureau of Investigation) and AMEX (American Express).

A **backronym** (my word, my definition) is sort of the opposite of an acronym. It takes a word, in this case your name, and uses each letter to make a sentence. Some people use this technique to memorize important things. In music, students learn the lines of the treble clef staff using backronyms: EGBDF—Every Good Boy Deserves Fudge.

Write your name—first, middle, last or full—as a backronym. (If you want a real challenge, try writing your full name as a single backronym!)

TRACEY
Tigers
Rarely
Are
Caught
Eating
Youngsters

ANN
Always
Nibble
Noiselessly

SCHOFIELD
Scholars
Comprehend
Hitherto
Obscure
Facts
In
Every
Lengthy
Dissertation

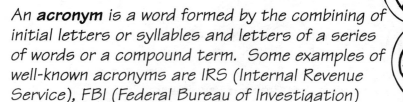

Activity 7

Backward Beast

*Spell the name of an animal backwards, creating a
new extraordinary and imaginary species.
Describe the animal: how it looks and behaves,
where it lives, what it eats.
(Your description can sound scientific or silly.)*

Scientific: The Noil: The noil (*Noilus subthermalus*) is found near subthermal vents thousands of feet below the surface of the Pacific Ocean. Because no light from above penetrates to this depth, the noil has no eyes. It does, however, have elongated, feathery antennae with which it senses movement in the water around it. This is presumably a mechanism of self-defense, as the noil is the staple of the *Shrimpus lionus* or lion shrimp, a voracious subthermal vent carnivore. The noil is invisible to the human eye. Under magnification, however, the noil's cylindrical, nearly translucent chest cavity exhibits a primitive heart and digestive system. While no one has ever witnessed a noil in the act of predation, the presence of incisors and an examination of stomach contents indicate that the noil feeds on bacteria that thrive in the heat of the subthermal vent. Because they are so difficult to study in their natural habitat, little is known about the noil's breeding habits. However, numbers suggest—each colony comprises several million animals—that it is an extremely successful species.

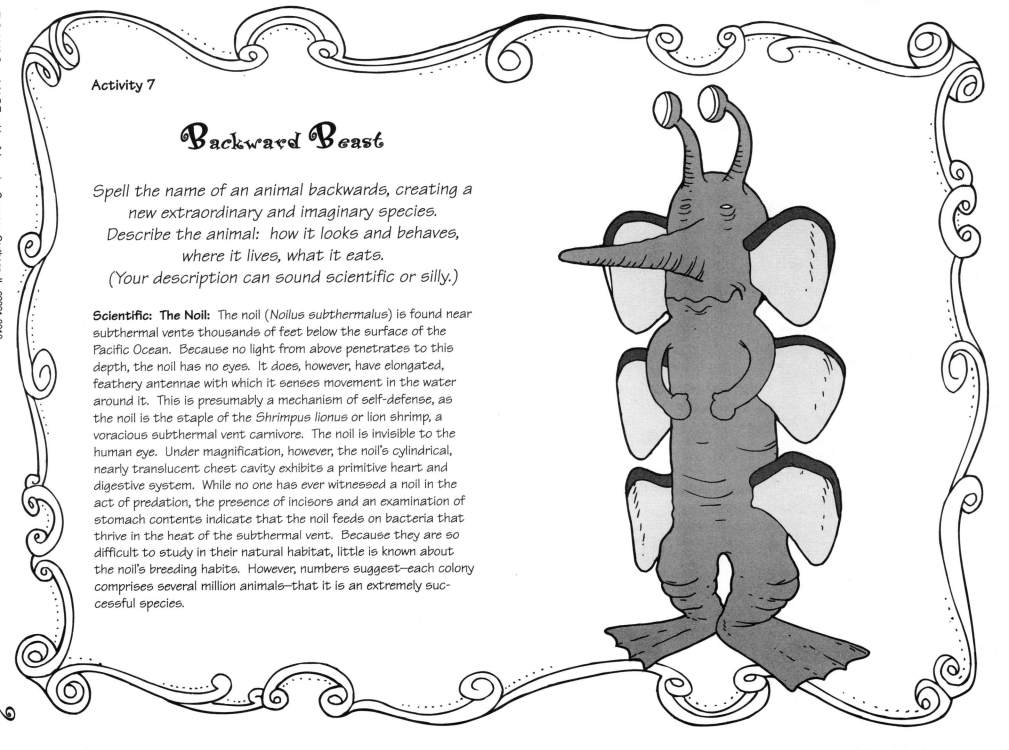

Backward Beast continued

Silly: The Noil: The noil lives on the Earth's moon. Noil burrows—the gigantic craters on the moon's surface—are made with the animal's huge, flipper-like feet. Its gray color (it blends almost perfectly with moon dust) makes it very hard to see, especially at night. It has very small eyes and seems to "hear" its way around with elephant-like ears that run in rows down either side of its body. It weighs 35 thousand tons and feeds on moon cheese, which it snuffles out of the dust with its 30-foot-long pointed nose. It eats an enormous amount of moon cheese each day—the equivalent of four billion cheese curds. The noil's diet contributes to its characteristically foul breath, which is noticeable at distances of greater than a mile. Noil babies are as large as blue whales at birth. These babies don't swim, of course, since there are no bodies of water on the moon, but wriggle about on their bellies like seal pups until they learn to control their front flippers and hump along in adult fashion. When full grown, noils will lump across the surface of the moon at about 20 miles per hour. Noils are quite vicious and attack with their flippers, savagely flinging moon dust into the eyes of their opponents during squabbles over food or territory—an aggressive maneuver that can cause blindness and even death. Being the only creature to inhabit the moon, noils have only one natural enemy—man. Although they are not carnivorous, noils have been known to kill and eat astronauts when provoked or threatened, especially in the breeding and calving seasons.

Bad Habits

Write about your worst bad habit.

My worst habit is slouching. I have slouched for so many years that I actually find it impossible to sit or stand up straight. When I try to straighten my back, I get short of breath and feel faint. This drives my husband—who equates good posture with self-discipline—crazy. He just doesn't understand. My whole family slouches. Generations upon generations of my family have slouched. You can see evidence of it in ancient family photos. My slouching habit is so bad that when I took horseback riding lessons as a child, my instructor made me wrap my arms around a broomstick that was placed behind my back to force me upright. This was not only uncomfortable, it was extremely embarrassing and undoubtedly contributed to my short equestrian career.

Believe It or Not

It is said that "truth is stranger than fiction." Think about the most outrageous "truth" or fact that you have ever heard. Write about it in your own words.

A man named Charles Osborne, who lived in Anthon, Iowa, hiccuped for 68 years straight! He began hiccuping in 1922 and did not stop until 1990 (when I guess he died). He never found a cure.

Guinness World Records 2000—Millennium Edition

Activity 10

Bottoms Up!

Think of a line or sentence that could serve as the conclusion of a poem or short story. Now write a poem or short story that ends with that line. (Hint: You can write forward and make the ending fit your story or backward and make your story fit the ending.)

Last Line
"And that is where she lives today."

Poem
Sally loved the ocean blue.
She loved to splash and swim and play.
She dove into Lake Timbuktu,
And that is where she lives today.

Story
In her mind Sally loved the jungles of deepest Africa. All her life she had dreamed of becoming a wildlife writer and photographer and studying animals in their native habitat. When she wrote a short story in public school, it was about lions. When she wrote an essay in high school, it was about lowland gorillas. When she wrote her thesis in college, it was about the complex ethical issues surrounding habitat protection, indigenous rights, poaching and the vanishing African rhino. The day Sally graduated from the University of Southern California with her masters degree in zoology, she boarded a plane for Africa. Setting up a small camp in the African jungle, Sally began to live her dream. And that is where she lives today.

Brain Drain/Brain Pain

*List five things you never want to forget
and five things you never will.*

I never want to forget . . .

   . . . the joy I felt when I first looked into the eyes of my
   newborn babies.

   . . . how it feels to be needed.

   . . . the love my parents have shown me.

   . . . my wedding day.

   . . . how lucky I am to be alive.

I will never forget . . .

   . . . the ridiculous dress and hairdo I wore to my junior
   high school graduation.

   . . . being sprayed by a skunk on the first day of high
   school.

   . . . "freezing" in panic while performing at a televised
   scholarship piano recital.

   . . . accidentally missing my grade 13 French mid-term
   exam.

   . . . the Christmas Day that my dog ate a
   four-pound box of Laura Secord™
   chocolates and then threw up 12
   times in 12 different places on our
   brand-new orange shag carpet.

Brokenhearted

*What broken or discarded toy
do you miss the most?*

I miss my doll, Cindy, the most. My mom and dad gave her
to me the day I was born. They called her Cindy because
that was the name they were going to give me before they
decided on Tracey. Cindy is still around in a box somewhere, but she has only a few strands of hair left. Her
head is all pockmarked with holes where hair used to be.
Her beautiful blue lidded eyes used to blink
when you picked her up and laid her down,
but now they are lashless and perma-
nently open, one all the way, the other
halfway, as if she has had a stroke. Her
stuffing is pretty much gone and her
soft plastic arms and legs hang spasti-
cally from her fabric shoulders and hips.
Her clothes have long-since disappeared, and her tan cloth body is
scarred with a big black patch.
When I see her, it makes me feel
sad, but I don't have the
heart to throw her out.
She is my childhood.
She is me.

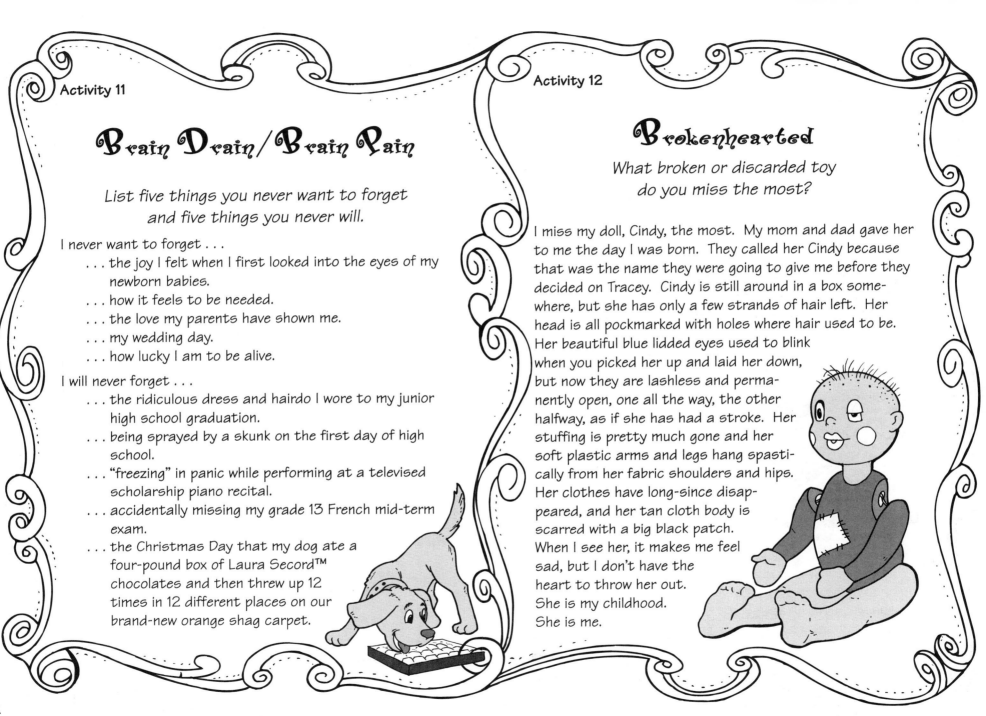

Activity 13

Cliff-Hangers

Write a paragraph that leaves the reader hanging. Now write several possible beginnings for the next paragraph. (Keep going if you want. Go back to the beginning and write forward to where you are or take the story to a conclusion and then think of the beginning. Who knows? You might just have something here!)

Time was almost up. If David didn't succeed in the next few seconds, he would have to go into hiding for the rest of his life. The sweat was pouring down his face, and his arms felt like jelly, but he refused to give up. Gathering all of his remaining strength, David gave one final, mighty push.

. . . The boulder gave under David's weight and went crashing down the hill, smashing into the terrorists' hideout and crushing the arsenal of weapons hidden within.

. . . The boulder didn't budge. David's life was over. Too exhausted to run, he slumped down at the base of the rock and prayed for a quick and painless death.

. . . The boulder went hurtling off the edge of the cliff taking David with it. He sailed through the air for a few feet, then plummeted to the ground, smashing into the rocky hillside and cartwheeling down towards the terrorists' hideout.

Congrats and Complaints

Write a paragraph or short letter . . .

. . . a. congratulating your parents on a job particularly well done or raising a complaint about something that could be improved on the homefront

. . . b. to your principal to commend the school team on an extraordinary effort or to lobby for change!

Wow, Mom and Dad! You sure have done a great job raising me to adulthood. You should be proud of yourselves. Thanks to all of the love and support you have given me over the years, I'm a published author. Now I have the opportunity to share all of the wonderful things you taught me and allowed me to experience growing up with a whole new generation of kids. Way to go!

Dear Principal Jenkins:

I wanted to bring to your attention an unfortunate situation that I would like rectified immediately.

As a result of the current bussing schedule, my two sons arrive at school 45 minutes early. School policy prohibits them from entering the building before 9:00 a.m. This means they are obliged to spend close to an hour outside, every morning, exposed to the elements. While I do not find fault with this situation for the most part, I do not believe it is reasonable or beneficial to their physical well being to be kept out-of-doors for this length of time in the rain or freezing cold.

I realize that early entry is against school rules and that granting this request might set an undesirable precedent, but due to the extremity of the circumstances, I would ask that you make an exception for my children in the case of inclement weather.

Thank you for your attention to this matter.

Yours sincerely,

Tracey Schofield

Activity 15

Constructive Critic's Choice Award

Write a review about the best or worst movie or book of the year, the best or worst professional sports outings in recent times, the best or worst fashions or styles of the rich and famous, the best or worst restaurant meals you have ever had or anything else you feel the urge to critique. (If you are being critical, make sure you offer some suggestions for improvement.
This is what constructive criticism is all about!)

And the Constructive Critic's Choice Award for Fine Dining goes to . . . The Emerald Mare! One of the best dinners I have ever politely devoured was at The Emerald Mare in Port Perry, Ontario. Overlooking a horseback riding stable, the restaurant specializes in fine dining in a relaxed yet elegant atmosphere. I ordered escargot as an appetizer—deliciously juicy with a rich garlic butter sauce!—and sampled my mom's savory cheesecake with bacon. Ooh la la! I was in a culinary paradise. Then came the mouthwatering main course—beef tenderloin with peppercorn sauce. The meat virtually melted in my mouth. The peppercorn sauce added just enough bite without overpowering the delicate flavor of the meat. For dessert? I somehow found room for hot apple dumplings in caramel sauce, the perfect sweet treat finale to a feast fit for a queen. The food was sumptuous and the overall effect splendid, although I did regret that there was no one riding in the arena that night. The vast earthen space below our window remained in complete darkness for the evening, which had a deleterious effect on the restaurant's ambience.

Would the critic return to The Emerald Mare for another meal? But of course! She has already been back twice to celebrate special occasions.

Constructive Critic's rating: 4.5 out of a possible 5.

Activity 16

Conversation Stoppers

Write a few sentences that are guaranteed to stop the conversation around you. (Try out your favorite at dinnertime and see if it works!)

I forgot to tell you, the police called while you were out last night.

Do you think it is fair that the principal gave me a three-day suspension for fighting today when I was just defending myself?

I failed my English test. In fact, I failed English.

Look at the hundred-dollar bill I found on the sidewalk today!

This letter says I have been named Student of the Year!

You know that $20 you gave me for my trip to the museum? I lost it.

Activity 17

Crazy Capers

Human beings often behave unpredictably, even foolishly. Some people are just plain nutty. Others are inclined to suffer from the occasional lapse in good judgment or common sense failure.

Write about two crazy capers: the craziest stunt you have ever heard about and the craziest thing you have ever done.

I can't imagine anything more crazy than going over Niagara Falls in a barrel. Have you seen those falls? Have you heard the water pounding down onto the rocks below? Have you seen the rocks below? The handful of people who have attempted this stunt must be insane. That some of them have braved (or "stupided") the falls, and survived to tell the tale, is a miracle. The fact that people are still trying to make the record books is testament to the truly quirky nature of humanity.

The craziest thing I ever did was to bring home a jar of six preserved rat embryos. I felt sorry for them when they

were removed from the womb of a female rat during dissection in grade 13 biology, so I filled a jar with formaldehyde and popped them inside. They were so tiny and pink and cute. It seemed cruel that they had been killed "in the name of science" before they had ever been born. I couldn't bear to see them thrown in the garbage or cut up and examined, so I took them home. I kept the jar on the kitchen counter for quite a while. I am not sure what happened to them in the end. I think my mom, who was an angel for putting up with me, finally must have become fed up with looking at them every time she was making dinner and quietly disposed of the jar while I was at school one day.

Activity 18

Creepy Crawly Characteristics

Think of an insect. Give it a proper name. Now imagine that your insect friend has a personality. Describe its creepy crawly characteristics and personality traits in detail.

Snider the Spider

Snider the spider is a sneaky, nasty little fellow. He builds a sticky net between two innocent-looking twigs and then hides out of sight, waiting for some poor fool to fly along and get stuck in his torture trap of doom. When this happens, Snider exhibits a frighteningly violent temper. He rushes out of hiding, grabs the trespasser by the throat and injects a poison into its body. Then while the poor thing is still alive, he sucks it dry of its life juices! If Snider is feeling a little full or not in the mood for body fluids, he wraps up the now-dead victim like a mummy and stashes it away for later consumption. Although his belly no longer clamors for sustenance, Snider repairs his snare and resets it! The tiny fiend then laughs a small but evil little laugh and scoots back into hiding. This is no longer about survival. Snider is very clearly enjoying his murderous activity. While he casually awaits his next victim, Snider pretends to read a book, but he never takes his eyes off the net. As soon as there is a little twitch or a wiggle, out he lunges, cackling wildly, brown hairs flying around him like a madman. Rubbing his eight little legs together with glee, he races off across the net and, without mercy, inflicts death once again.

Activity 19

Cut-and-Paste

*Cut out individual words, and short paragraphs if
desired, from an old newspaper. Glue them onto
a piece of paper in such a way as to construct
a new and interesting or silly sentence
or paragraph.*

A man was hit by a dog today as he
was walking his car to school. The man
was uninjured, however the dog
sustained a bullet wound to its left
foot. The car was taken to the
hospital by ambulance but was
pronounced dead on arrival and
impounded. It will be buried on
Tuesday.

Activity 20

Dictionary "Un"definitions

Pick out a strange-sounding word from the dictionary—one that you have never heard before. Don't look at the definition. Now make up your own definition of the word. Try to make it sound believable. Compare your definition to the real one. Which sounds more plausible? Read both definitions to a friend and see if he or she can guess which is correct. (If you are in a goofy mood, try a silly definition instead of a serious one. Or, try two definitions for the same word: a serious one and a silly one.)

Word: trangam

Dictionary "Un"definition:
(serious)
a lengthy journey by rail
(silly)
the act of transferring money from one's savings account to one's checking account in support of a gambling habit

Dictionary Definition: a knickknack

Word: wase

Dictionary "Un"definition:
(serious)
a length of rope knotted at both ends
(silly)
a small piece of food which, having fallen from the mouth during the action of impolite chewing, now clings annoyingly to the shirt front

Dictionary Definition:
a wisp or bundle of hay

Activity 21

Emotional Outbursts

Describe an emotion (happiness, sadness, anger, fear, joy, rage, jealousy, admiration, loneliness, insignificance, elation, hunger, love, hate, tranquility, contentment, creativity, exhaustion, excitement, disappointment, etc.)

How does it make you feel?
How does it make you act?

Actions

1. When I am happy, I am nice to everybody. I want to give my mom and dad presents and tell them how much I love them. When I am happy, I draw pictures with lots of bright colors.

2. When I am angry, I am mean to everybody. I make my mom and dad feel bad telling them terrible things that I really don't mean. When I am angry, I break my crayons and make scratch marks on all my best pictures.

Feelings

1. Happiness enfolds me like a pair of soft, warm hands. It breathes sweet air into my lungs and inflates me gently until I feel like I might burst into joyous song. Happiness lifts me high up into the air and holds me there, above the mountaintops, above the clouds and lets me dance in the heavens like a ballerina in the satin folds of a star-encrusted music box.

2. When I am angry, the world is black all around. My heart is darkness and my soul is night. I live in a lightning-struck tree, smoldering in the raging storm, thrashing like an ill wind in the branches of the living.

Activity 22

Extraterrestrial Rewrites

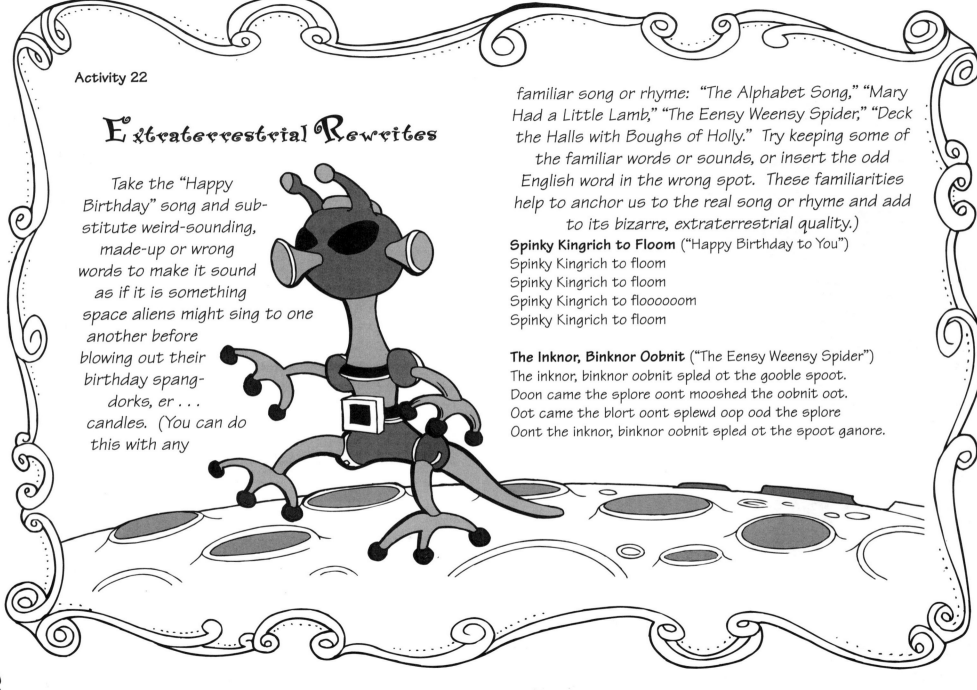

Take the "Happy Birthday" song and substitute weird-sounding, made-up or wrong words to make it sound as if it is something space aliens might sing to one another before blowing out their birthday spang-dorks, er . . . candles. (You can do this with any familiar song or rhyme: "The Alphabet Song," "Mary Had a Little Lamb," "The Eensy Weensy Spider," "Deck the Halls with Boughs of Holly." Try keeping some of the familiar words or sounds, or insert the odd English word in the wrong spot. These familiarities help to anchor us to the real song or rhyme and add to its bizarre, extraterrestrial quality.)

Spinky Kingrich to Floom ("Happy Birthday to You")
Spinky Kingrich to floom
Spinky Kingrich to floom
Spinky Kingrich to flooooooom
Spinky Kingrich to floom

The Inknor, Binknor Oobnit ("The Eensy Weensy Spider")
The inknor, binknor oobnit spled ot the gooble spoot.
Doon came the splore oont mooshed the oobnit oot.
Oot came the blort oont splewd oop ood the splore
Oont the inknor, binknor oobnit spled ot the spoot ganore.

Activity 23

Fact to Fiction

Take a simple fact and distort it. Make your fictional "fact" sound believable, like a way-out report you might hear on the radio or read in a tabloid newspaper.

Fact: An electric pencil sharpener is used to sharpen pencils.

Fictional "Fact": An electric pencil sharpener is used to sharpen pencils. But did you know that these useful gadgets can also be used to sharpen the mind? In a recent study at Distortion High School in Gotcha, Pennsylvania, grade 12 students who sharpened pencils for five hours a day over a one-month period actually increased their average math scores by 10 percent. Students who did not sharpen pencils saw less than a two-percent increase in their math standings in the same period.

Activity 24

Famous First Words

What would you say if you came face to face with your favorite actor, sports star or all-time hero?

"I have been dreaming of this moment my entire life. In those dreams I never sounded foolish. I did not perspire. I was not rigid with fear. I did not shake uncontrollably. I asked intelligent questions that indicated my abiding interest in your professional achievements. I was mildly overwhelmed by your presence, but I did not gape or fawn. Above all, I was in complete control.

"Instead, I find myself a puddle at your feet: gaping, fawning, shaking uncontrollably, rigid with fear, perspiring profusely and babbling like an idiot. Please forgive me. My world is small, and you have been such a large part of it for so many years that I find myself reduced to mere atoms in your presence. Having admired you from a distance for such a long time, I am utterly unnerved by this sudden intimacy. I am sure that if you give me just a few hours I will recover my composure and we can engage in normal discourse. More than anything I would like the opportunity for us to have a conversation in which we each play the role of a rational human. Maybe then we can for-

get all about the crazed and unscripted monologue that is presently gushing forth from the mouth of an overwhelmed and incoherent fan and freezing to the spot the presumably embarrassed object of her admiration and affection."

Activity 25

Fantastic Flotsam*
and Jetsam**

Pretend you have just found an object from a shipwreck floating in the water at the ocean's edge or washed up on shore. Write a short paragraph describing the object, where it came from, what it was used for, who owned it/used it and the fate of the owner/user.

The head of the porcelain doll was surprisingly well preserved. Other than a small hole in its cheek, (and the fact that it presumably had been severed from a porcelain body of similar fate) it showed no real signs of distress. The head lay in a cradle of sand, and the black eyes stared up into mine as if begging me to stay and listen to their sad story.

Suddenly, the image of a beautiful little girl with a head of blonde curls came swimming before my eyes. She was swinging a porcelain doll in the air, whirling across the deck of a great ship. Dancing to the music of a fresh start, the little girl and her doll floated across the wooden slats

on a gust of hope and the promise of freedom. Were they sleeping when the ship foundered?

Does the little girl now lie in a watery grave clinging to the body of her delicate companion?

I pick up the doll's head and gently slip it into my pocket. I will take it home with me, and they will live on my flotsam and jetsam shelf together: the porcelain doll, the little girl and their dream of a better life.

*flotsam: Goods cast or swept from a vessel into the sea and found floating.
**jetsam: Unbuoyed goods cast from a vessel in peril, and which sank.

Flying High

Where would you go if a private jet (or spaceship!) could take you anywhere in the world (or universe)?

I would hop into a rocket ship and blast off to the moon for a few days. I'd really love to look down on the Earth from outer space, but I wouldn't want to go too far from home. (I don't think I could stand more than a couple of days of dehydrated astronaut food, no bathrooms and zero gravity!) A lunar getaway seems like the perfect solution for a homebody looking for a little intergalactic adventure.

Food for Thought

Think of your favorite food.
What do you associate with this food?
How does it make you feel when you eat it?
When do you crave it the most?

Of all the foods in the world, I like doughnuts the most. Doughnuts make me think of lazy Saturdays with my family, of jammies and cartoons and ice cold milk. When I eat doughnuts, I feel like I am easing back into a big, soft, comfy chair with my feet up and my slippers on. I feel warm and full and contented. I crave doughnuts the most when I have had a really hectic week and things seem totally out of control. When I'm really hankering for a doughnut, I know it's time to slow down, get back to the basics and enjoy the little things in life.

Activity 28

For Sale

Write an ad for something you would like to put up for sale: your used pencil crayons, your out-grown bike, your old comic books or CDs, your house, your smelly sneakers, your dinner, your pierced ears, your goldfish . . . your brother.

For Sale

One slightly used husband. Good with children and pets. Diminished income-earning potential. Comes with mid-life crisis, expensive sports car and clothes on back. No offer too low. Call during football season (ask for long-suffering wife) at 437-9677 or HES-YORS!

Activity 29

Fridge-id-Air

Make a descriptive list of the 10 most interesting (or disgusting) things in your refrigerator or freezer.

Items in My Fridge

1. skim milk (or watered-down chalk)
2. nasal passage-searing extra hot horseradish
3. liquid vegetable (paraded as celery in past life)
4. ancient mystery meat in mud-brown coagulate
5. very hairy carrots
6. something fuzzy and green and probably really smelly (last year's turkey)
7. container surprise (a.k.a. leftover tuna sandwich)
8. red and sticky puddle on bottom shelf with relish jar hostage
9. extra old cheddar supporting thriving penicillin colony
10. shrink-wrapped, dehydrated half-cantaloupe that bears a striking resemblance to Great Uncle Art without his false teeth

Activity 30

Future Flyers

*Describe the vehicle you will be "driving"
in the future. Draw it.*

Fifty or so years from now, I will be piloting a Hovercar.
This small, insect-like commuter vehicle will hold a driver
and single passenger. It will have the ability to "float"
over established roadways, creating a second traffic
tier and easing congestion. The Hovercar will feature
jet-powered boosters that complement a conventional
electric-powered drive train, giving the car the ability to
maneuver on the ground as well as in the air. With
"glide-on-the-fly" capability, the Hovercar will allow dri-
vers to make dangerous last-minute observation-based
decisions regarding the *road least travelled* and select
the most efficient transport mode in a matter of micro
seconds. (It will also make parking a heck of a lot easi-
er.) Hovercars will come in a variety of pleasing colors
and the basic version will cost slightly in excess of
$150,000. Leather interior, air conditioning, power win-
dows and rocket booster upgrades will be available. Bud
vases will come standard in every Hovercar.

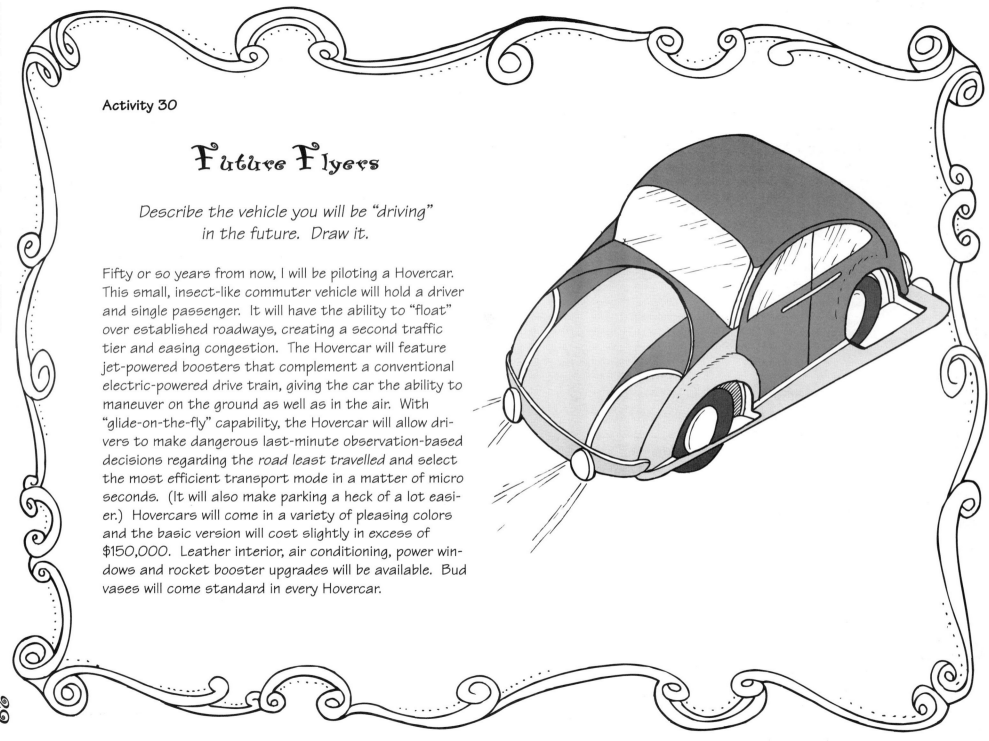

Activity 31

Garage Sale

Write a descriptive list of 10 things that you should get rid of from your closet or toy box.

Because I am a pack rat by nature, this is a very difficult exercise for me. In the name of efficiency, organization and "the five Ss"—sort, sweep, simplify, standardize and self-discipline—I should probably get rid of at least the following items (and this is just stuff from my bedroom closet):

1. my size 10 wardrobe from 1985 B.C. (Before Children)
2. the birthday cards I have been saving since I was six
3. my boxes of costume jewelry
4. three pairs of worn-out fuzzy slippers
5. a couple of my five housecoats
6. the winter sweaters I wouldn't dare to wear
7. at least a hundred pairs of socks
8. my dainty pink wedding shoes (my post-wedding feet are a good three sizes bigger)
9. a large percentage of my stuffed animal collection (which numbers in the thousands)
10. all of my panty hose that have runs in them

Activity 32

Give Me One Good Reason

Actually, 10 good reasons why . . .
. . . bears should be allowed to sleep all winter
or . . . you should be allowed to stay up until
midnight on Saturday
or . . . homework should be illegal
or . . . turkeys should never be left outside in the
rain
or . . . computers should replace handwriting
or . . . you should be allowed to work to music at
school
or . . . learning should be accomplished by osmo-
sis while you are sleeping
or . . . weekends should be five days long, week-
days only two

or . . .

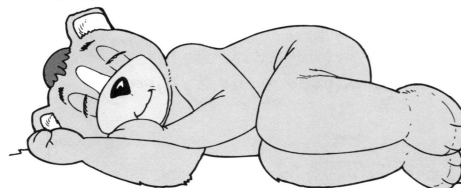

Give me 10 good reasons why pugs are such darned cute little canines.

1. Because they act like little people, not little dogs.
2. Because they snort and snuffle when they breathe.
3. Because they tip their heads to the side when you talk to them.
4. Because they don't come when you call them (In a pug, even obstinacy is endearing.).
5. Because they have a little curlicue for a tail.
6. Because they don't walk, they prance.
7. Because they have bulgy little eyes like Marty Feldman.
8. Because they run around and around in a tight circle when they are excited.
9. Because they are so wrinkly.
10. Because they are such an improbable—almost surreal—creature.

Activity 33

Goofy Get-Togethers

Think of two things that have absolutely nothing in common. Write a compelling reason why they might actually belong together.

A ballet slipper and a lumberjack

Before his mother died and his father moved the family up north to the logging town of Akidnodreamdo, Big Ben the Lumberjack (then known as Little Ben the Ballerina) entertained thoughts of the national ballet school and a career of dance. Without a studio nearby, Ben wilted under intense paternal pressure, put away his dreams and his slippers and picked up an axe. (He still keeps the slippers in a little shoe box in his cupboard with a picture of his mother.)

A teacup and a baseball bat

A washed-up circus clown—who based his entire, worn-out comedy act on the balancing of a stack of glued-together teacups on a baseball bat—keeps a teacup and a bat on a shelf in his old circus trailer home to remind him of better days.

TLC10240 Copyright © Teaching & Learning Company, Carthage, IL 62321-0010

Activity 34

Grandiose Good-Byes

Write a farewell letter to your best friend,
your school, your old sneakers . . .
your cheese sandwich.

Good-bye, dear pencil stub. You were a true friend and a constant companion. I will miss your pointy little graphite nose and your rubbery little head. I used to love sticking you in the pencil sharpener when you were dull and watching you pop out as good as new after a few quick spins of the handle. I will never forget the words we wrote together: the homework, the tests, the notes to our classmates. We had some good times. Although you will soon be replaced by another, you will remain in my work and heart forever. I hope you enjoy your new home in the garbage basket.

I sign here with you for the last time.
Your friend and master,
Tracey

Activity 35

Greatest Gifts

*Write about the best present
you have ever received.*

My three children are the greatest gifts I have ever received. Matthew, Patrick and Stephanie have given me more joy than I thought it possible to experience. Sometimes my heart is so full of love for them that there is no room left in my chest for breathing. I cannot imagine living in this world without them.

Whew. That was a bit heady. On the material side, I suppose the best present I have ever received was the antique walnut bedroom suite my parents gave to my husband and me as a wedding gift. It has three pieces: a mirrored chest of drawers, a kidney-shaped dressing table and a double bed with head- and footboard. Although the chest of drawers is a bit small for all of my clothes, the dressing table is a bit small for my teddy bear collection and the bed a bit small for a family of five, I can't imagine getting more use, or pleasure, out of a gift. Thanks, Mom and Dad.

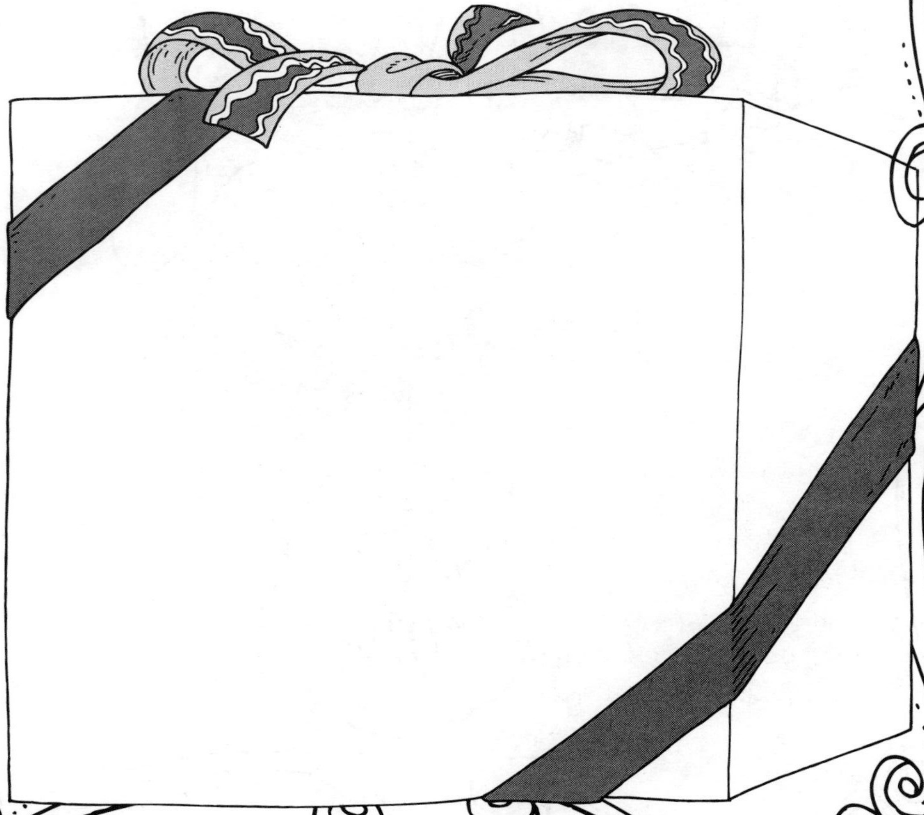

Activity 36

Greetings, Fellow Earthlings

Write a creative greeting for an answering machine.

Greeting 2

Greetings, fellow earthlings. Yoo have greeched 333-3333. The Dleigochs cannot commba to the floon root noo. Please leave yoor noom oonnd floon noombro, and they will claw you root bewk. Good nooktno oond hoov a ploosant oomrow.

Greeting 3

Ello-hay. Ou-yay ave-hay eached-ray e-thay ofield-Shcay esidence-ray. E-way are-yay aking-tay ig-Pay atin-Lay

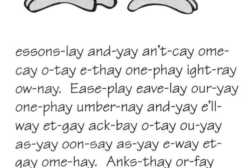

essons-lay and-yay an't-cay ome-cay o-tay e-thay one-phay ight-ray ow-nay. Ease-play eave-lay our-yay one-phay umber-nay and-yay e'll-way et-gay ack-bay o-tay ou-yay as-yay oon-say as-yay e-way et-gay ome-hay. Anks-thay or-fay alling-cay.

Greeting 1

Ugh! You've reached the Schofield cave. We can't take your call right now, we're probably out clubbing our dinner to death or running for our lives from a ferocious meat-eating dinosaur. Please leave your name and number, and we'll get back to you as soon as we can . . . If we can.

Activity 37

Halloween Sugar Highs

Describe your favorite Halloween candy.

As a kid, my favorite Halloween candies were the tiny little two-packs of Chiclets™ gum. I especially liked the red and yellow ones—cherry and lemon. Yum, yum. They were so sweet. Too bad they lost their flavor after a few minutes, and you had to keep eating more. I always traded candy with my brother so I could get a big stack of those color-ful boxes. Sometimes my mom let me take a pack to school in my lunch bag to chew at recess or on the way home. I can taste them right now, just thinking about it.

Activity 38

Happy Holidays

Write about your happiest holiday memory.

When I was a kid, my family would travel the country for several weeks each year. Sometimes we would go north. Sometimes south. Sometimes east or west. Although we had a lot of really neat adventures whenever we parked our homemade camper and went exploring, we had some of our best times on the road. While Dad was driving, my brother and I would play drawing games, taking turns adding body parts to strange creatures or making sense out of squiggles. And we would all sing songs together like "Down by the Bay" and "My Eyes Are Dim" and "They Say That in the Army." We ate on the fly, grapes and sand-wiches and stuff that my mom had packed before we set off each morning. When we got tired, my brother and I would put a pillow between us and rest our heads together so we could sleep comfort-ably upright. I don't think I ever felt more like a family than when the four of us were rolling down the highway on our way to a brand-new place.

Health Hazards

*Write why homework, chores, detentions, etc.,
are hazardous to your health.*

Doing the Dishes

Doing the dishes is hazardous to my health because it hurts my back. I am tall and the sink is too low in the counter. (What was wrong with the ergonomist who figured out the sink height/back strain relationship, anyway?) I have to stand almost doubled-over just to get my hands into the water. And then I have to bend over there for hours, scouring and scrubbing and aching. I keep stretching just to get the knots out of my poor lower back muscles. And, of course, there's all the twisting and turning. That can't be good for your tendons and ligaments. Bend and wash, twist and rinse, straighten and drain. It's a physiotherapist's nightmare. I can almost hear my sciatic nerve screaming at me to "Please stop! Have mercy!"

And my hands! My waterlogged hands are like prunes when the water finally swirls down the drain. It doesn't last, though. That would be a blessing. No. As soon as they air out, my hands turn as dry as the Sahara Desert. Dishwashing costs me a fortune in hand lotion and moisturizers and still I have bleeding, cracking, chapped hands. Rubber gloves aren't the answer, so don't even mention them. I can't wear rubber gloves because they make me drop stuff, and I can't afford to break any more dishes. And, of course, the water has to be just below the boiling point to get rid of all the bacteria. I'm surprised I don't get blisters! I suppose I shouldn't complain about dry, dishpan hands—it's better than first-degree burns.

And what about that drain basket! Cleaning the little egg bits and cheese strings and unidentifiable vegetable orts out of that thing just about makes me vomit. I can't even face my food at dinner because I know that later on I'll be scraping the drain with my fingernails. No dinner, however, means late-night snacking which contributes to my weight gain and disimproves my overall well-being. I don't think there is any doubt: doing dishes is positively, absolutely hazardous to my health.

Activity 40

Home Remedies

Write a home remedy for the common cold, a headache, sibling rivalry, parental disapproval, homework overload, "chore-itis," etc.

Home Remedy for Care Giver (a.k.a. Mother/Wife) Burnout

1st Cancel any breakfast, lunch and dinner engagements.
"Sorry, kids, you'll have to get it yourselves."

2nd Engage the services of a certified domestic engineer.
"Is this Maid for You? Great. I'll see you in an hour."

3rd Do not take any calls.
"That can't be for me. And if it is, I'm not here."

4th Do not receive any visitors.
"I'm going to my room now. Don't open the door unless Ed McMahon is on the front steps with a check for a million dollars."

5th Order in room service.
"Honey, can you bring me a tray and some of that dinner you're cooking?"

6th Relax.
Aaaaah. A good soak in a hot tub.

7th Enjoy.
Mmmmm. Under the covers with a good book.

8th Hang the "Do Not Disturb" sign on your bedroom door.
*Sleep in late. Close the curtains. Don't set the alarm. Even if the house next door explodes, **do not** get out of bed.*

9th Hold yourself hostage.
Tell your family members that if they don't pitch in and help, they will never see you again.

10th Repeat steps one through nine whenever you are feeling unappreciated.

Activity 41

Hospitable Homonyms*

*Think of a pair of homonyms.
Use both words in a single sentence.*

fair, fare

fair: an occasional or periodical exhibit of articles of value or interest

fare: food and drink

I went to the International Food Fair and sampled exotic fare from around the world.

Reid, read

Reid: a boy's name

read: to apprehend the meaning of something printed or written

Reid Stanley likes to read fantasy books about white knights, damsels in distress and great, fire-breathing dragons.

*homonym: A word identical in pronunciation to another but different in spelling and meaning.

TLC10240 Copyright © Teaching & Learning Company, Carthage, IL 62321-0010

Activity 42

How Are You?

Although "How are you?" is the standard greeting between acquaintances, the question is largely rhetorical.* The person asking the question is not really interested in the state of the other. He/She is merely soliciting the courteous response, "I'm fine. How are you?" Throw polite society a curve ball. Write down what you would say if you were to answer the "how are you?" question in detail. (Your response can be truthful or fanciful.)

When Things Are Going Very Poorly

"Actually, I'm really awful. My goldfish died this morning. I'm on my way to school to take a history test that I haven't studied for. It's February. I hate the cold. I have Seasonal Affective Disorder and get incredibly depressed every year at this time, but for some reason it seems to be especially bad this year. I have no money. I haven't had a good night's sleep in weeks. I am eating like a horse, and I've gained at least 50 pounds since Christmas. All my friends are going south for March break, and I'm stuck here in the land of ice and snow. I lost my wallet yesterday and my last five bucks. But other than that, I'm just dandy. How are you?"

*rhetorical question: A question put only for oratorical or literary effect, the answer being implied in the question.

How Are You? continued

When Things Are Going Exceedingly Well

"I'm great! I can't believe how well things are going for me. I'm at the top of my class this year and have just been awarded a scholarship to the university of my choice. I just got back from a wicked week-long skiing trip in Vermont, and I met the most incredible guy. My parents are taking the summer off work, and we're going to travel in Europe for two months. My grandparents are giving me $500 spending money and buying me a whole new wardrobe for the trip. Physically, emotionally, academically and socially, I have never felt better. I'm working out three days a week, and I'm incredibly fit. I made the volleyball and basketball teams, I'm chair of the yearbook committee and I'm the drummer for the stage band. I volunteer in a shelter for the homeless and at the nursing home where my grandmother lives. I'm unbelievably popular at school. I have so many friends I can't fit them all into my busy schedule and so many invitations that I have to pick and choose between them. My teachers say that I'm the best student they have ever taught, and they are sure that I'm going to be super-successful at whatever I choose to do with my life. My peers just selected me valedictorian and *Teen People* named me Teen of the Year. I'm going to be on the cover of the magazine next month with Leonardo DiCaprio. How are you?

Activity 43

Human Beans

Use personification* to make your sneaker, your house, your peanut butter sandwich, your dog or any other nonhuman thing or creature seem hominoid (human-like).

Human Beans

I smiled delightedly as the two little brown beans swaggered around in my hand, swaying to the strains of some silent symphony. Like tiny ballerinas, one suddenly leapt into the air while its companion did a perfect pirouette on my palm. Momentarily overcome by gravity, the two collided, fell back on their heels and then sprang up again in unison.

Roll over, Rover . . . I Mean Fred

The stray dog looked around the cage and winked one little brown eye at his kennel companions. He had behaved so politely and had taken such care to hide his imperfections that he felt certain the little girl would take him home. He held his leash in his mouth expectantly, and happily swept the floor with his tail while he waited for her to say the word that would open the doors to freedom.

*personification: Makes a comparison in which something that is not human is described in human terms.

Activity 44

If I Were a . . .

*Make a list of 10 unrelated objects. Think creatively
and use each one of them in an
"If I were a . . . I would . . . " sentence.*

If I were a . . .

1. . . . shoelace, I would tie myself in knots for you.
2. . . . bookcase, I would offer children stories of unimaginable depth and beauty.
3. . . . teddy bear, I would snuggle a child to sleep every night.
4. . . . flower vase, I would be full to overflowing with daisies.
5. . . . computer, I would check myself for viruses each and every morning.
6. . . . box, I would contain the most wonderful present.
7. . . . cupcake, I would be covered in thick chocolate icing and rainbow sprinkles.
8. . . . lizard, I would lie in the sun all day and listen to the crickets sing.
9. . . . battery, I would bring a cordless telephone to life.
10. . . . pocket, I would be deep and filled with countless children's treasures: foil, crumpled paper, small stones, half-eaten candies, pennies, shiny things, bits of string and broken rubber bands.

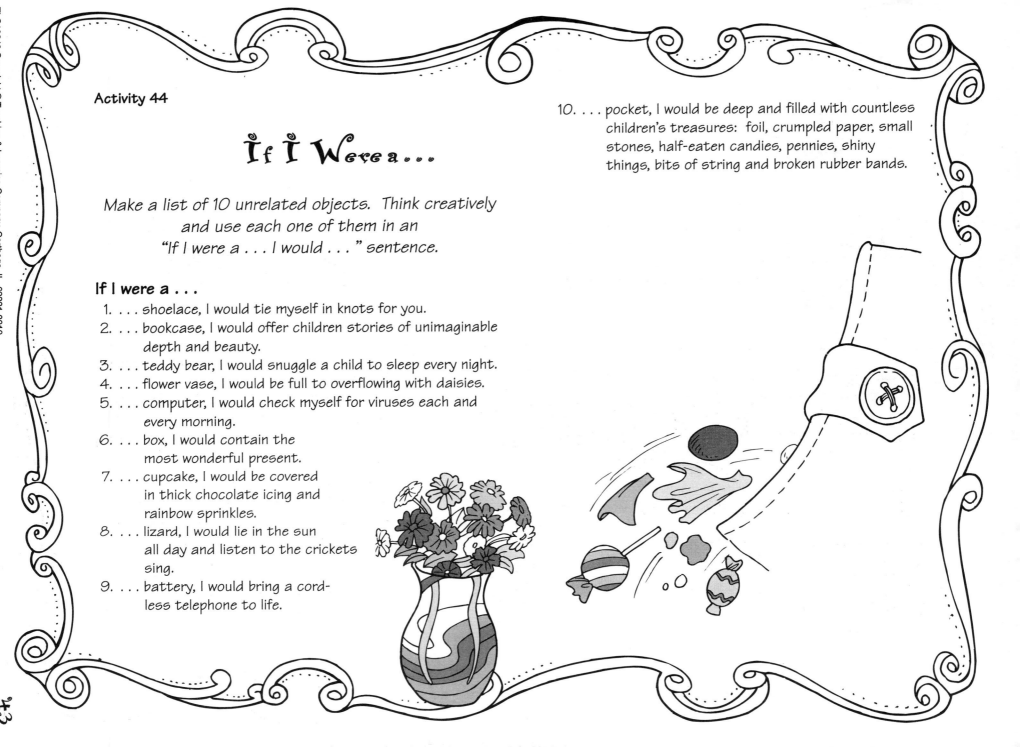

Activity 45

In the News

Write at least the first paragraph of a news story using a headline from a newspaper or magazine. Don't read the story before you write your article.

Park Officials Shut Barn Door—Before the Animals Leave*

Dwingdom: Park officials in Dwingdom County have closed the petting farm at Dwingdom Acres Park, but have no idea what will happen to the animals. Approximately 70 animals that resided at the park are now without permanent homes and are being housed temporarily at the Dwingdom County Animal Shelter.

The decision to shut down the farm was made by park officials after they received repeated complaints that the animals—some 25 ducks and chickens, 20 goats and sheep, 10 rabbits, 6 pot-bellied pigs, 3 donkeys, 2 cows, 1 llama and a Capuchin monkey named Pierre—were being mistreated. The farm, which is situated on leased land within park boundaries, is owned and operated by an independent party.

According to Warden Darren Thomas, the parks department would like another owner/operator to assume the Dwingdom farm and its 70 domestic animals, but he is not optimistic. Should the farm remain closed, Thomas hopes that a petting farm of good repute in a neighboring county will purchase the animals, which are reported in fair health.

Meanwhile, the shelter is struggling to accommodate its unexpected guests and is asking for donations of food and for volunteers who will tend to the animals while their fate is being decided. An official police investigation into the matter is pending, and no formal charges have been made. Anyone with information regarding the matter is asked to contact the county sheriff.

*This headline appeared in the January 20, 2000, edition of *The Globe and Mail*. The story that accompanies it here is purely fictional.

Park Officials Shut Barn Door

Activity 46

Inviting Invitations

Write an invitation to "the party of all parties."
Make it sound so incredible
that no one would want to miss it!

On Friday, February 14, the Wawanessa Glee Club will hold its 150th annual Valentine's Dinner and Dance—on a Boeing 747! Party goers will boogie the night away at 30,000 feet on their way to Paris, France, for a weekend of fun and frolic in the land of amour. Take your sweetheart on the trip of a lifetime this Valentine's Day and give a gift of love he or she will never forget. Tickets for this spectacular event are limited to 100. Take advantage of the Glee Club's incredibly low airfare and accommodations package. Reserve your seats before Friday, January 12, and receive a complimentary meal deal that includes dinner and drinks at two of the finest restaurants in the City of Lights.

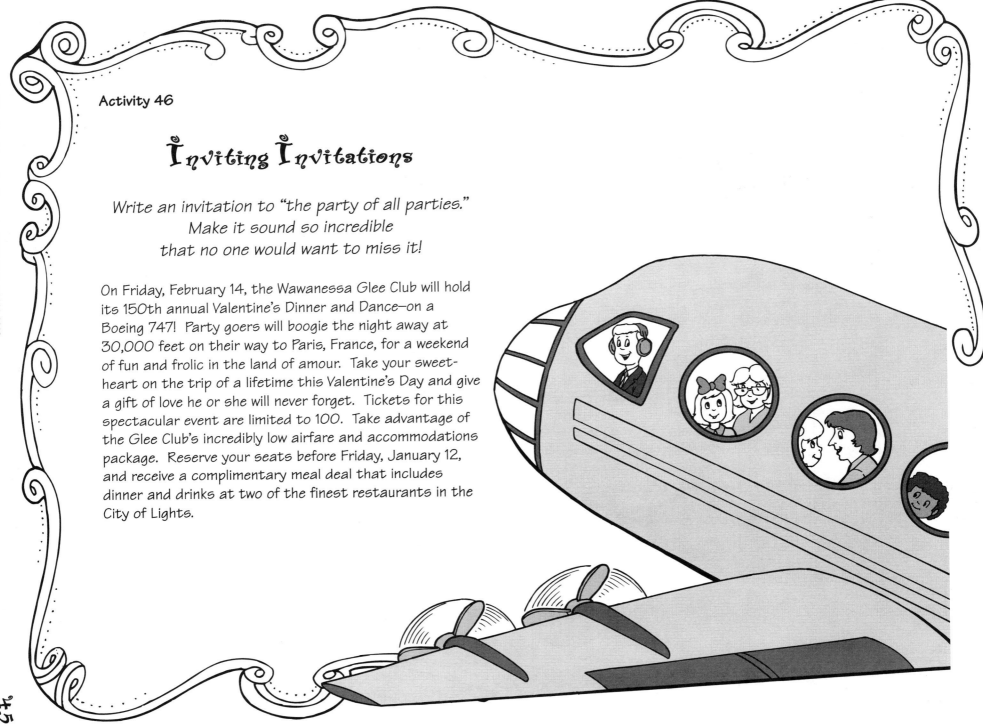

Activity 47

It's Me! And It's Perfect

Describe how you have personalized your bedroom to make it your own. What would you add/change to make the room say, "It's me! And it's perfect"?

What I Have Done

My bedroom is full of antiques and teddy bears. It is painted a rich caramel color and has sliding doors that open onto a country porch and a beautiful forest. I have pictures that my kids have drawn hanging on my dresser mirror, and on the dresser top in aged silver frames I have black and white photographs of my parents when they were little and on their wedding day. Two brush and comb sets—one belonging to each of my grandmothers—are displayed with love on my dressing table. My wedding picture sits on my bedside table, which is a burned and water-scarred antique chest belonging to a sailor on a WWI warship. My grandmother's cedar chest sits at the foot of my bed adorned with stuffed toys.

What I Would Do

To make my bedroom even more "me," I would have a floral comforter on my (king-sized antique brass or distressed pine) bed or perhaps a handmade quilt in soft greens and browns and creams. I would have matching shams on enormous pillows and complementary throw cushions and bolsters. I would hang original watercolors on my walls in gold gilt frames. I would put brocade window toppers and horizontal wooden blinds over my sliding doors. I would also add a treadmill, a color television and a stereo!

Activity 48

Join the Pros

If you could join your favorite sports team or musical group, which one would it be and why?

Sports

I would join the Olympic Equestrian team, because I love horses, and I love riding and grooming and touching and smelling and just being around equines. (Also, I would have to be an expert horsewoman in order to join these incredible amateur athletes in international competition—something I am certainly not and would love to be.)

Music

I would not like to join an existing musical group. I would like to be the lead singer for a brand-new band. I would like to tour the U.S. with a great new act—not opening, but headlining—and set the world on fire with a completely different new country sound. (Of course, I would have to get over my terrible fear of performing in front of others first!)

Activity 49

Lottery Longings

*What would you do/buy if you won
10 million dollars in a lottery?*

If I won 10 million dollars in a lottery, I would immediately put enough in the bank to keep me living the rest of my life in the style to which I would quickly become accustomed. Then I would take my family to Disney World for a two-week all-inclusive vacation. I would travel Europe with my husband and my parents (and my kids if we could take along a live-in nanny). Every winter I would fly to a new and exotic destination to enjoy hot sun, warm sand and clear blue water. I would buy my husband a Lotus Elise (his favorite car of all time), snowmobiles for my whole family and dirt bikes for my two boys. I would buy a horse that we could all ride and a few goats for my daughter because she loves feeding animals and goats appear to be insatiable. I would buy my dad a four-wheeler, a bigger lawn tractor (with a mulching deck) and a pond. I would build my mom an addition on her log house and fill it with a huge, new kitchen crafted from hickory. I would hire a maid service to do all of my housework and find a great caterer who would prepare a few meals for my family every week. I would also buy a new van—one with slid-

ing doors for passengers on either side of the vehicle (and a windshield that cracked.) I would hire a contractor to extend the main floor of our house so that my eldest son could sleep upstairs with the rest of us, and I could have an office with a window. I would also have someone build us a new—safe—deck on the back of the house and an accessible path down to the river. Finally, I would buy a boat—or maybe a yacht—which would easily house my extended family. (And then I would pay someone to find a cure for motion sickness so that I could actually set foot on it without vomiting!)

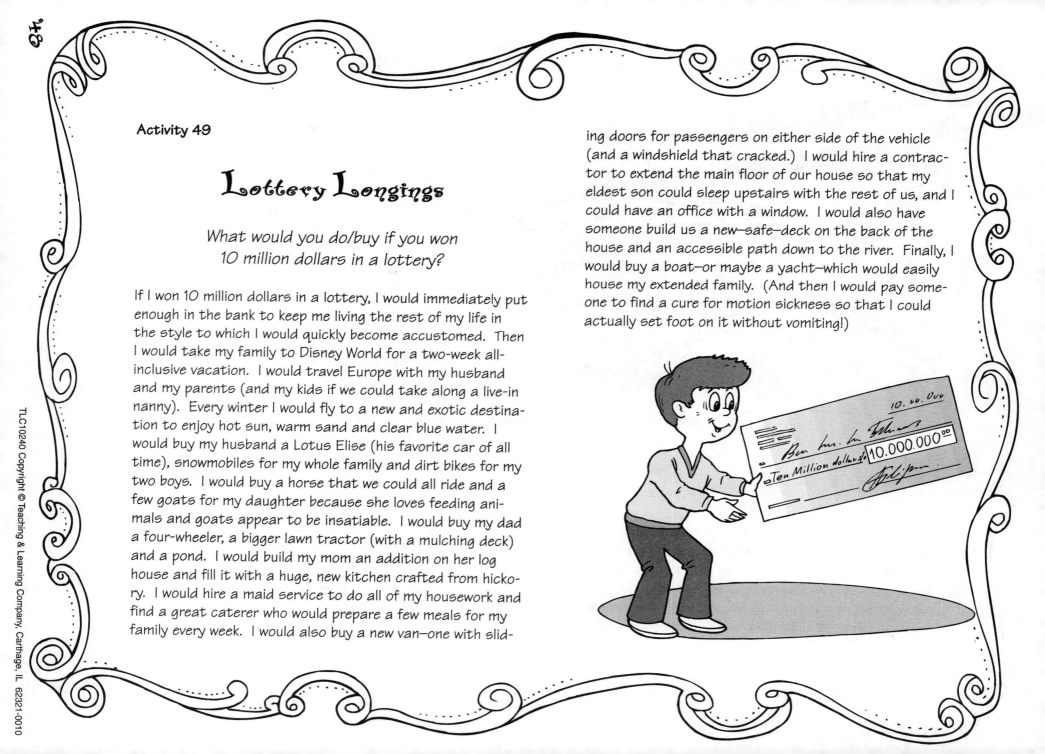

Love/Hate Relationships

Write about the things you love and hate the most.
(They can be two different things or
opposite sides of the same coin!)

I Love Dogs

I love dogs. I love big dogs, mostly, but I also love pugs. I love the way they thump their tails when you talk to them (or wiggle them in the case of the pug). I love the way they run to greet you when you get home. I love the way they gallop down country roads in the fall when the leaves are golden and orange and red. I love the way they lick your face (when their breath is good) and your toes when your feet are tired. I love the way they sigh when they are contented. I love their cold, wet noses. I love the way they get so excited when it snows for the first time each year. I love the way they roll over to have their bellies rubbed. I love the way they bark and make you feel protected and safe. Most of all, I love the way they keep you company when you are all alone and lonely.

I Hate Dogs

I hate dogs. I hate the way their hair gets on your clothes and in your food. I hate having to scoop their poop and clean up their barf when they eat plastic containers or rubber chew toys. I hate their muddy footprints all over my clean floor. I hate the way they run away and won't come back when you call them. I hate the way they chew furniture and strew garbage all over the street. I hate feeling responsible for their happiness and then guilty when they don't get enough attention. I hate the way they pull so hard on the leash they knock you right off your feet. I hate the way they take up so much room in the car. I hate having to pay their vet bills, and I hate buying them 25-pound bags of food that last only a couple of weeks. Most of all, I hate the way they get old and die and leave you alone when you have grown to love them like a child.

Activity 51

Making Headlines

Read an article in a newspaper—without looking at the headline. Now think of at least five titles you might give the story. (If one of your headlines grips you in a creative fever, go with it! Write a new story based on your terrific title.)

A doctor wrote the story I read. It was a reflective account of a late-night housecall to pronounce the death of a 67-year-old man in the presence of his two sons. It was entitled, "The Housecall: A doctor's stream of consciousness." It appeared in the January 20, 2000, edition of *The Globe and Mail*. Reading the article made me think of these possible titles:

- A Night for Remembering
- Stranger in a Dead Man's Bedroom
- Go Silently into the Night
- For the Love of the Father and the Sons
- The Last Visit
- Cracks and Creases and a Neat British Gentleman
- Reflections in a Broken Mirror
- The Death Certificate
- A Life Unravelled

A Night for Remembering

Go Silently into the Night

Ficticious News

A Life Unravelled

Activity 52

Maniac Menus

How would the menu at Cannibal's Cafe read?
What would be the bill of fare at the Doggie Diner?
What would they serve at the Jurassic
Kitchen—favorite eatery of Mr. Theodore Rex and
other insatiable carnivores? Think up a maniac
menu for your favorite fantasy foodery.

The Cat's Meow

Appetizers
Mouse tails in a savory rodent sauce
Vinegared fish tails
Minced mole morsels

Entrees
Mousetrap surprise
Fishy filet in a tangy lemon butter sauce
Rat-a-tat-touille
Chicken fingers

Desserts
Chocolate mouse mousse
Creme de la creme de le creme brule
Beef 'n' liver quiver
Porksicle

Beverages
Saucer of warm milk
Tuna-juice in a tin
Eau de toilet

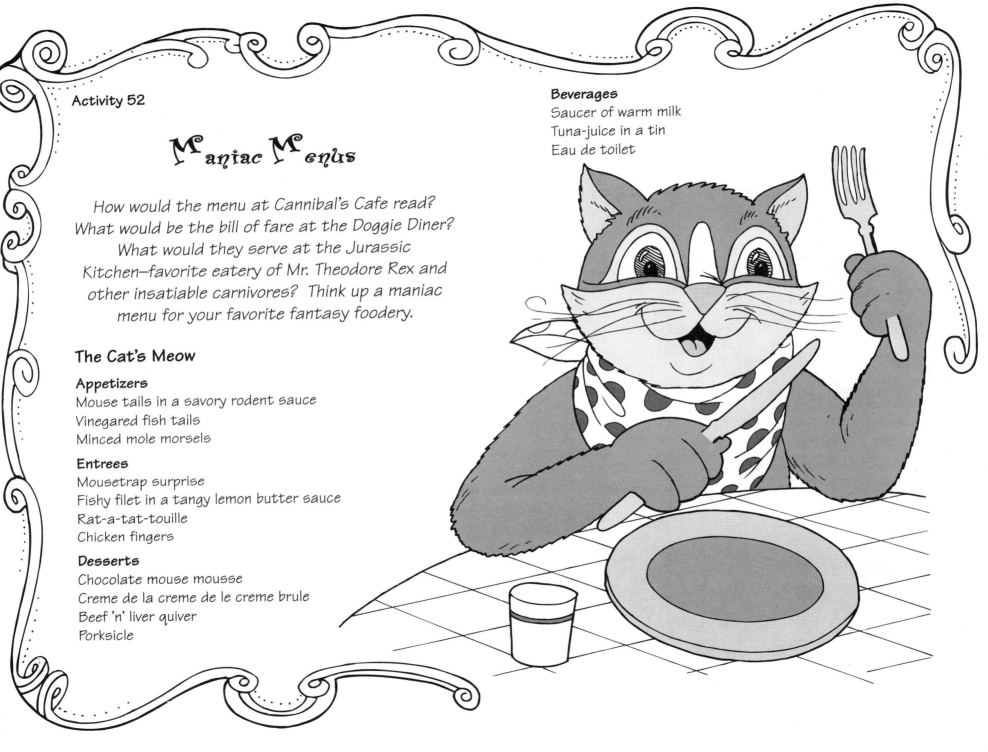

Activity 53

Meal Mysteries

Describe the contents of your dinner without actually naming the food items on your plate. (Take your "meal mystery" to school and see if a friend can figure out upon what you supped.)

My Meal Mystery

Appetizer
Confused green leaves avec une wardrobe spectaculaire (mixed salad with French dressing)

Entree
Ground up dead cow pressed into a rectangular baking pan and cooked (meat loaf) with a snowman's broken, blistered nose (chopped, cooked carrots); whipped white root with eyes removed (potatoes); slimy, green instant-muscle maker (spinach)

Dessert
Round, flat discs, baked to a golden brown and filled with sweet brown lumps (chocolate chip cookies)

Beverage
Liquid calcium (milk)

Activity 54

M_{is-m}Ādages*

(-m-Axioms**, -mAphorisms*** and -mApothogems****)

Rewrite some of the adages on the next page by changing one or more words shown in the brackets. Be creative with your new endings. Make them sound moralizing, profound or silly. (Try creating a number of mAdages from the same adage. Try mixing two adages together.)

Profound/Moralizing

- One man's garbage is another man's livelihood.
- United we stand, divided we meet in the boardroom to discuss things rationally.
- What's good for the goose is good for the goose's troublesome brother.
- The bigger they are the harder they are to tickle in the armpits.
- There's no place like the back of the bus.

Silly

- If you can't stand the heat, get out of the sauna and roll around in the snow for a while.
- If you can't stand the heat, get your sneakers out of the fire.

- If you can't stand the heat, get central air.
- If you can't stand the heat, get out of your snowsuit.
- If you can't stand the heat, get the heck out of Arizona.

Mixed

- If you can't stand the heat, get out of the frying pan. (32 & 37)
- Children should be seen and not hasty. (1 & 9)
- A picture is worth a thousand sleeping dogs. (19 & 42)
- Don't put all your eggs in one ear. (30 & 31)
- Too many cooks throw the baby out with the bathwater. (24 & 33)

*adage: a saying that has obtained credit or force by long use; a proverb
**axiom: a self-evident or universally recognized truth
***aphorism: a brief statement of a truth or principle
****apothogem: a terse, instructive, practical saying

Mis-mAdages continued

1. More haste less (speed).
2. Haste makes (waste).
3. One good turn deserves (another).
4. Don't put the cart before the (horse).
5. Never put off until tomorrow what you could do (today).
6. One bad apple spoils the (bushel).
7. Don't cry over spilt (milk).
8. The bigger they are the harder they (fall).
9. Children should be seen and not (heard).
10. Silence is (golden).
11. Hindsight is (20/20).
12. What goes around comes (around).
13. There's no time like the (present).
14. Absence makes the heart (grow fonder).
15. Never look a gift horse in the (mouth).
16. It's better to have loved and (lost) than never to have loved (at all).
17. Smile and the world smiles (with you); cry and you cry (alone).
18. An apple a day keeps (the doctor away).
19. A picture is worth a thousand (words).
20. A teaspoon of honey helps (the medicine go down).
21. He who laughs last (laughs best).
22. A stitch in time saves (nine).
23. Waste not (want not).
24. Too many cooks spoil the (broth).
25. Spare the rod and spoil the (child).
26. Feed a cold, starve a (fever).
27. Home is where (the heart is).
28. There's no place like (home).
29. Don't count your chickens (before they hatch).
30. Don't put all your eggs in (one basket).
31. In one ear and (out the other).
32. Out of the frying pan and into the (fire).
33. Don't throw the baby out with the (bathwater).
34. Do unto others (as you would have them do unto you).
35. Beauty is in the eye of the (beholder).
36. You can't judge a book by (its cover).
37. If you can't stand the heat, (get out of the kitchen).
38. What's good for the goose is good for (the gander).
39. The way to a man's heart is (through his stomach).
40. What goes up, must (come down).
41. Cream always rises to the (top).
42. Let sleeping dogs (lie).
43. United we stand, divided (we fall).
44. Truth is stranger than (fiction).
45. You never miss the water (until the well runs dry).
46. One man's garbage is another man's (gold).

Missing

Write the text for a poster that describes a missing person, animal or thing. Describe who, or what, is missing: its name, appearance, habits, last known location, etc. (Illustrate your poster.)

MISSING!

One orange-kneed tarantula. About 10 inches in diameter or the size of a small dinner plate. Classroom pet. Very tame. Does not bite but will "throw" hairs when excited or nervous. Black with eight orange-spotted legs and lots of eyes. Answers to the name of Hairy. Last seen in terrarium in Mrs. Ark's grade 4 class. If found, please handle with gloves and place in sealed container with air holes. Return as soon as possible. Warning! Tarantula has not eaten for several weeks and *will* be hungry! Do not place near pets or small children.

Movie Mania

Look in the entertainment section of the newspaper and write down at least five current movie titles. (If you don't have a newspaper, think of some of your favorite movies or ask a friend for suggestions.) Use the titles in a sentence, paragraph or short story.

Movie Titles

Snow Falling on Cedars
Stuart Little
Any Given Sunday
Man on the Moon
The Green Mile

Sentence

It is winter in Seagrave and, on any given Sunday evening, you can see Stuart Little walking the green mile of his backyard fence, chatting happily to the man on the moon and watching the snow falling on cedars that he has planted as a buffer against the encroaching city.

Activity 57

My How You've Changed

Interview someone who is quite a bit older than you to find out how things have changed since he or she was a kid.

Interview with My Mom

- There were no electric refrigerators when I was little. We had a wooden icebox at the bottom of our cellar stairs to keep our food cold. The iceman came once a week to deliver one of the big sawdust-covered blocks of ice that he carried in his truck.

- The milkman delivered milk and butter to our door every morning in his horse and cart. If we put two empty glass milk bottles on the porch, he left two full bottles. In the winter, if you didn't get right out to bring in the bottles, they would freeze. When you got to them later, the little paper lids would be sitting up on top of a chimney of cream.

- We used to buy our meat fresh from the butcher. Ten cents worth of cooked ham fed my whole family lunch. And candy! You could buy so much candy for 25 cents that two girls could make themselves sick eating it all. Of course, everything was a lot cheaper then. You could buy a new Model A Ford for $500 and a three-bedroom house, with a huge backyard, for less than $3000.

- When you got sick, the doctor went to your house—in the middle of the night or whenever. There was no health care insurance. People paid the doctor cash for his services. I had my tonsils out on the kitchen table. My mom helped the doctor and my goldfish died from the ether they used as an anesthetic.

- Entertainment was a lot different. We bought a black and white television when I was about 13. We could get two or three channels. Radio was very popular. Families would listen to weekly shows like *Amos and Andy* and *The Shadow*. My parents never went out. They had friends over for singsongs every Friday night. On Saturdays, I used to go to the movies. A double-feature, plus cartoons, cost 25 cents. I went by myself. Parents never worried about letting their kids go out alone. There was very little crime.

- Communications have changed dramatically. We had a rotary dial telephone, but we never made long-distance phone calls. We wrote letters. And, of course, we had no computers—no internet.

Activity 58

Name Game

What do you wish your parents had named you? Why? Which of your nicknames do you like the best? If you were going to be an actor or a novelist, what stage name or pen name would you give yourself?

Different Name

I have grown quite attached to my name and don't really wish to be known by any other. However, if they were doing it all over again, I think I would like my parents to call me Emma-Lee Maynard (a variation of my paternal grandmother's middle name, Amelia; and my maternal grandmother's maiden name, Maynard). I like the old-fashioned sound of that name, and it suits my antique-crazy, family-crazy personality.

Favorite Nickname

My favorite nickname? "Muggabil" or Muggy for short. I have no idea how or why my husband came up with this one, but it kind of stuck. When I was pregnant with our first child, we nicknamed it "Muggy Junior," not knowing if we were having a boy (which we did) or a girl.

Pen Name

When I was younger and fantasized about sidelining as a romantic novelist, I thought I would write under the pen name, or pseudonym, "Ashton Cavanaugh." (Having divulged my secret identity here, I guess I'll have to accredit my romantic writing to a different "nom de plume"!)

Activity 59

Number Poems

In a number poem, each digit represents a line of the poem—and indicates the number of words in the line. Try writing a number poem using your birth date and any theme that takes your fancy. Substitute the number five for any zeros. (You can write number poems using any number: your telephone number, the number below a bar code, your street number, today's date, your zip code, your Social Security number, the ISBN number on this book . . . .)

My Birth Date: 05/20/63
Line 1: 5 words (5 substituted for 0)
Line 2: 5 words
Line 3: 2 words
Line 4: 5 words (5 substituted for 0)
Line 5: 6 words
Line 6: 3 words

My Birth Date Poem
Writing
Relentlessly plumbing heart and soul, (5)
Writing is a healing act. (5)
Expressive, revealing—(2)
a pathway to the spirit—(5)
writing is about searching deep inside (6)
and bursting forth. (3)

Activity 60

Ode to Joy (or Yesterday's Leftover Tuna Casserole)

Write an "ode": a lofty rhymed or unrhymed lyric poem (one which is based on the poet's feelings and emotions rather than reason) that builds upon a single dignified theme. Your theme can be elegant or a little rough around the edges.

Dignified Theme, Unrhymed
Ode to the Morning Sun

Looking out my window to the east
I am struck by the bright beauty of your face as it sets
   fire to the horizon.
The sky is painted in soft strokes of pink and orange that
   overtake the night as you ascend slowly to the heavens
   and bathe the world in your light.
Your son, the moon, has escaped to his western bedroom
   leaving you alone on your celestial throne to rule the
   universe of a morning on Earth once again.

Undignified Theme, Rhymed
Ode to a Shoe

Oh little shoe I write for you
An ode of humble praise.
Although I hold that truth be told
We've both seen better days.

Your wear doth tell you've served me well
Oh garment once so bright.
Your eyes grow dim your leather slim
And yet you hold me tight.

Your sole is true my little shoe
Despite its dingy face.
Your tongue regales a thousand tales
Of brighter time and place.

Your tread is worn, your canvas torn
Your laces tattered, too.
The road's been rough, you've had enough
Alas! I know you're through.

So here's to you my trusty shoe
Without you I go bare
And limp the Earth with little mirth
And blisters everywhere.

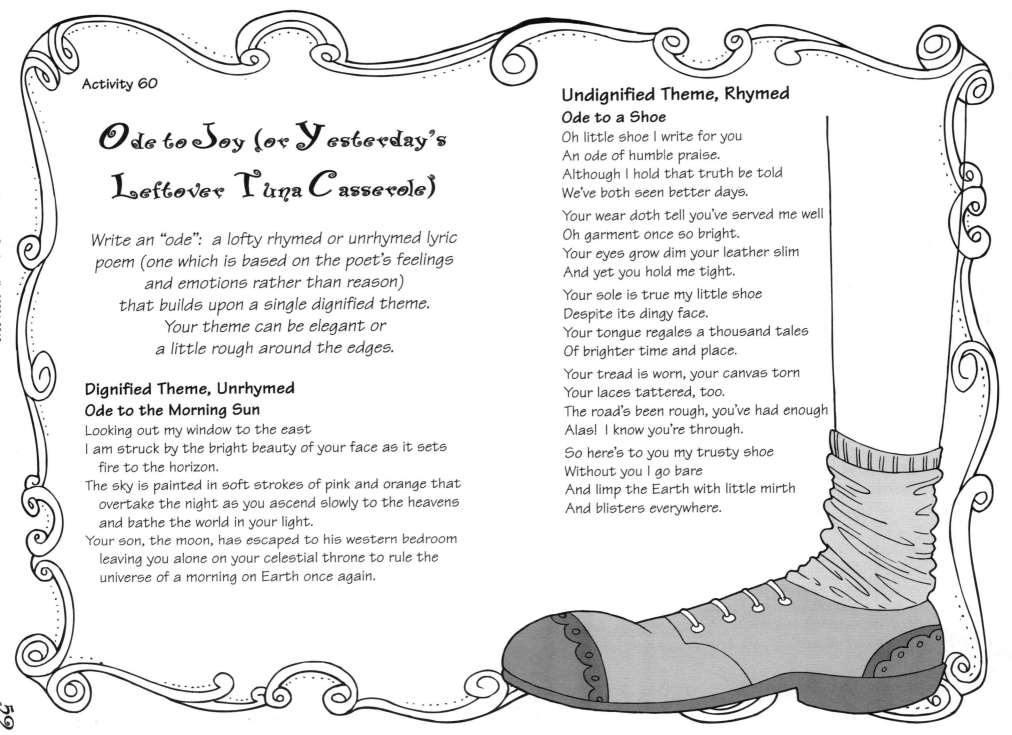

59

On the Spot

Ask a friend to give you a topic—the weather, your favorite shirt, the different ways in which elephants use their trunks . . . anything at all—and write for two to five minutes about that topic without stopping to think or to make any additions or corrections. The important thing here is not the quality of your writing, but your thought process, the kindling of your creative fire and the transfer from brain to paper of the uninterrupted stream of your consciousness.

Roller Coasters

When I was little, my grandmother used to take me on The Flyer at the Canadian National Exhibition. It was the oldest roller coaster in Canada; wooden and rickety and surely unsafe. Grandma was a tiny, gray-haired lady even then, but she loved the thrill of the ride. I would squeeze in beside her and the two of us would take off on a two-minute thrashing: slamming from side to side as the car cannoned through 45 degree twists and turns; screaming and holding onto the lap bar

for dear life as the car plummeted down what seemed to be a sheer vertical drop. When we disembarked, breathless with exhilaration, Grandma would line up again and take my brother. By the end of the day her little stick legs were covered in bruises from repeated violent contact with the sides of the red metal car, but she never seemed to notice or to care. I think she would have been disappointed if we had been too afraid to go.

As a grown-up, I took my own young children on amusement park roller coaster adventures. The kiddy kind. From the beginning Patrick loved the speed and the feeling of danger and the rush of wind in his face. He has a lot of his great-grandmother in him. Matthew was more hesitant, refusing to accompany Patrick and me on the Log Flume at Canada's Wonderland because the Ghoster Coaster had terrified him so badly. Emboldened by the passage of time, however, Matthew now loves the big boy rides—the upside down, loop-the-loop, backwards and forwards roller coasters that suck the breath right out of you and hurl the contents of your stomach back up into your mouth. This kind of derring-do is too much for his motion-sick mother. I keep my feet firmly planted on terra firma and get dizzy watching him exult in the aerial acrobatics of The Bat and Top Gun and Drop Zone. If only his great-grandmother were still alive. I'm sure she would be a game companion, white hair, bruises and all.

Activity 62

Outlaws

Write about something that you feel should be illegal. Provide a persuasive argument to support your belief.

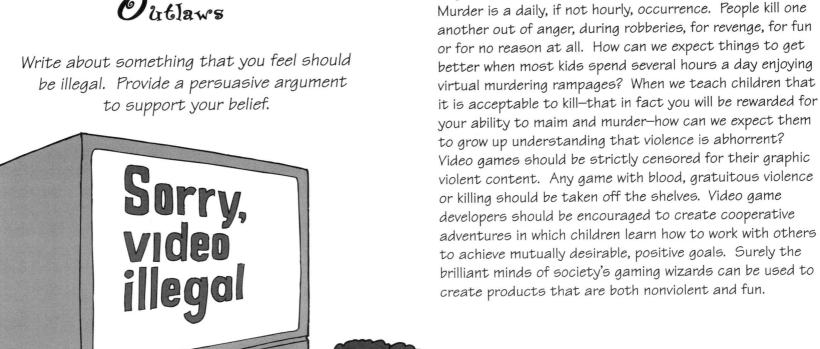

I think that excessively violent video games should be illegal. Our society has become so focused on violence. Murder is a daily, if not hourly, occurrence. People kill one another out of anger, during robberies, for revenge, for fun or for no reason at all. How can we expect things to get better when most kids spend several hours a day enjoying virtual murdering rampages? When we teach children that it is acceptable to kill—that in fact you will be rewarded for your ability to maim and murder—how can we expect them to grow up understanding that violence is abhorrent? Video games should be strictly censored for their graphic violent content. Any game with blood, gratuitous violence or killing should be taken off the shelves. Video game developers should be encouraged to create cooperative adventures in which children learn how to work with others to achieve mutually desirable, positive goals. Surely the brilliant minds of society's gaming wizards can be used to create products that are both nonviolent and fun.

Activity 63

Oxymoronics

An oxymoron brings contradictory terms sharply together for emphasis. The silly song "Oh, Susannah" is a study in such contrasts.

"It rained all night the day I left
The weather was so dry.
The sun so hot I froze to death
Susannah, don't you cry."

Write an "oxymoronic" (my own term) sentence or paragraph that makes excessive use of oxymorons.

I stared into the bright black depths of the ocean. There, staring back at me with unseeing eyes, was the biggest shrimp I had ever seen. It was stunningly grotesque—a beautiful monster—and it swam towards me with the awkward elegance of an ungainly ballerina.

Activity 64

Pet Peeves

Write about the annoying habits of your pet or the pet that you would like to own.

My cat, Anniken, is the nastiest, most persistent creature I have ever known. She rubs all around your legs, friendly-like, and then, when you go to pick her up, she swats you across the face with her paw. She bites children and she growls deep in her throat—a rumbling, threatening sound—when anyone goes near her. She is an outside cat, a mouser, but whenever you try to open the door, she runs in, searching for food. She has an insatiable appetite. When I am unloading groceries, she leaps into the trunk and starts chowing down on anything she can get her fangs into. She even ate a workman's lunch and a box of doughnuts one day last summer.

She loves vehicles almost as much as she loves food. An open door is an open invitation, and she has the scar to prove it. (A crook in the end of her tail is visible evidence of a stowaway attempt and a hasty—and hefty—door closure.) We literally have to jump out of our van and slam the door shut or she's in. And if she does manage to sneak by security, she goes into hiding immediately and won't come out. She has been trapped inside a vehicle overnight (foraging for leftover snack food) on more than one occasion. She even likes to ride on top of cars. And once she gets on, she won't get off. You can drive away down the road, and she stays glued to the spot like a furry hood ornament. Even sudden braking won't dislodge her. Unless you want to take her with you, you have to stop the car and physically lift her off. Then you have to throw her (gently but a good distance) from the car, jump back in and speed away or the whole cycle starts again.

Activity 65

Pick Me! Pick Me!

If you had to leave your house in a hurry and could take only one thing with you, what would you choose?

I would take my photo albums. (This is a little cheaty, since I have more than one!) Pretty much everything else I own could be replaced, but not the pictures in those albums. I have always had a terrible memory, and presumably it will only worsen with age. Even now, the only way I can remember what my kids were like when they were little is by looking at the photographs I took of them in each of their precious stages. I can't imagine growing old without those albums. They are a frame-by-frame documentary of my life as a mother. I would be utterly bereft without them.

Picture This

Look at a picture, a painting or any other decorative piece of art in your home or school. Describe it: how it looks, how it makes you feel. Name it.

The Barn on Daisy Hill, a watercolor by Norma Dixon

At the top of a green hill that is awash with daisies sits a cream-colored barn with a red tin roof. The barn—doors and windows open to the spring air—is sheltered by a lone tree not yet in leaf. The sky is tufts of blue and yellow. The whole painting is soft pastels, giving the impression of fresh, new life on a sunny day in early May. The painting makes me feel tranquil and lighthearted; it always has. Looking at it I can almost feel the cool grass on my bare feet, smell the hay in the barn. I feel youthful again, like a child in a field of wild grass playing "He loves me, he loves me not" with the white petals of a daisy.

Pizza Party

Draw a large triangular pizza shape. Draw some of your favorite pizza toppings on the triangle. In each topping, write one of the "ingredients" of your best-ever birthday party, family birthday or the birthday party of your dreams.

My Best-Ever Birthday Party

Pepperoni:	Eight good friends
Olive:	Eight great gifts
Green Pepper:	Seven seats for musical chairs
Tomato:	Twenty layers of newspaper wrapping on one special prize
Onion:	One blindfold, one tail and one donkey
Jalapeno Pepper:	One tub of vanilla ice cream
Ham:	One big, round chocolate cake with sprinkles, candles and my name in curly letters
Pineapple:	One precious dime, wrapped in cellophane and tucked into the middle of the birthday cake

Activity 68

Point and Shoot

Open a book to a page somewhere in the middle. Close your eyes and touch your finger to the middle of that page. Use the sentence that your finger is touching to write a few sentences or paragraphs of a news story.

"The mother bear smiled to herself."*

She loved the way her twin cubs curled together when they slept. They looked so peaceful, so comfortable together. When they were awake, all they did was fight.

Granted, their rough and tumble was helping them to gain the skills they would need to survive in the wild without her. Still it was annoying. What was it about boys? Were they born quarrelsome?

Looking at them now, the curve of Illiwack's back pressed tightly into the hollow of Agulark's belly, their incessant squabbling was difficult to imagine. She wished the days could be like this, quiet and peaceful and free of bickering.

Annuloogah licked the inside of her son's ear and little

Illiwack stirred. He yawned and stretched and dug his foot into Agulark's thigh.

"Mom, he kicked me!" cried Agulark, instantly awake and ready for battle.

"Come on, boys," said Annuloogah, rising stiffly to her feet. "It's time to get dinner." She sighed, resigning herself to her fate as a mother of two small rivals. So much for peace and quiet.

*Starter sentence from *Let's Write! Grades 4-6* by Robynne Eagan and Tracey Ann Schofield, published by the Teaching & Learning Company, 1999.

Activity 69

Promises I Mean to Keep

Make a list or 10-page booklet of promises for a friend, a pet, a parent, a sibling, a snowman, a lunch bag, a library book, an elbow pad . . . .

Promises to My Laundry Hamper

Promise 1:   I promise to throw my dirty clothes into you every night.

Promise 2:   I promise that, if I am using you like a basketball net, I will pick up my fouled "balls" and stuff them.

Promise 3:   I promise never to put wet towels in you.

Promise 4:   I promise to carry you to the laundry room and dump you out every Friday night.

Promise 5:   I promise to keep you hidden in my closet at all times (except on Friday nights when I take you to the laundry room for dumping).

Promise 6:   I promise never to use you as a cage for my cat.

Promise 7:   I promise not to hide my brother's toys in you.

Promise 8:   I promise never to give you pants that have belts or stuff in the pockets.

Promise 9:   I promise not to take clothes back out of you and wear them to school.

Promise 10:   I promise never to force-feed you any clean clothes. (You know, the ones that I just don't feel like folding neatly and putting away in my dresser drawer.)

Activity 70

Promises, Promises

What promises do you keep making—and breaking?

I keep promising myself that I will take the time to exercise and to get in shape. I also keep promising myself that I will quit drinking so much cola and work on improving my poor eating habits. I make these outrageous promises to myself every day, pretending that I will be able to muster up the willpower to change, yet knowing that I am too deficient in self-discipline to live my life any differently. Maybe tomorrow. Maybe next week. Yeah, right. Maybe in another lifetime!

Activity 71

Pushing the Limits

Write on one subject, pushing the limits of believability until you find yourself way over the top and deep into the world of fantasy.

A Whale of a Tale

When I was little, I used to go fishing at my grandpa's cottage in Vermont. (Believable) It was a beautiful place. (Sure, why not?) Twenty rooms in all. (Questionable) More of a mansion, really. (Doubtful) I had my own bedroom. (Maybe) It took up the whole fifth floor. (I don't think so) I could see all the way to New York City from up there. (No way! Impossible)

The cottage was on this huge bottomless lake. It was filled with fish. And I mean filled. You didn't have to use a fishing pole. Just a net. You could scoop the net into the water, and it would come up full of fish. Fish of all shapes and sizes and colors. Freshwater fish, saltwater fish, even sharks! Once I caught a small whale in a net that was as big as our boat. The whale was so strong it pulled me right out of the boat and down into the water. Down, down, down I went until there was no more light. There were fish all around me, bumping into me, smacking me with their tails as if to say, "You don't belong here!" I kept holding on to the net. Even though I was almost out of air, I couldn't let go. Then, out of the great blackness, a huge whale came gliding toward me. It was the baby's mother.

And she was pretty mad. I could tell by the look in her tiny eye. She stared right at me for a full minute, giving me a silent scolding with that dark little eye, and then she opened her huge mouth and swallowed me whole. It was dark inside, and it smelled like fish, but I wasn't scared. I could breathe again. She was full of oxygen. As I bumped around in her enormous belly, she began to rise toward the surface. And suddenly, with a great rush of water, she spurted me out of her blowhole. I landed with a plop in my grandfather's boat. Boy was he surprised! He wanted to give me a great big hug, he was so glad to see me, but I stunk so badly that all he could do was hold his nose and smile. We never saw the mother again, but every so often, for years afterward, the baby whale would pop back up to the surface, catching fish with my boat-sized net and giving me a wink with his little black eye.

Activity 72

Retail Sales

*If you were a door-to-door salesperson,
what product or service would you sell? Why?*

Since you can't buy happiness even if you *could* put a value
on it—and that would be my ware of choice—I suppose I
would peddle cameras and film. As the old adage goes, "a
picture is worth a thousand words." Everyone should have
a means of capturing forever life's most precious
moments. I would be doing people a great service by pro-
viding them with the technology necessary to compile a
visual archive of their family history. Reminiscing about
"the good old days" brings people great joy at every stage
of life, and the passage from one generation to the next
a catalog of photographs is one way to ensure that the
greatest moments of one's ancestry—the happy ones— are
never forgotten. I guess, in a way, by selling these particular goods, I *would* be selling happiness.

Scavenger Hunt

Design your own scavenger hunt. The items on your list can be down-to-Earth and "gatherable" or the fanciful stuff of daydreams and fairy dust. Give your scavenger hunt a suitable name.

The Movie-Goer's Scavenger Hunt

1. a movie ticket stub
2. a newspaper movie listing
3. a popcorn kernel
4. a picture of a movie star
5. a movie review
6. the name of one song from a feature film
7. the telephone number and address of a theater near you
8. the names of three major motion picture studios
9. the title of one upcoming feature film
10. the name of one Academy Award-winning Best Actor, Best Actress and Best Picture

The Hunt for Cinderella's Happiness

1. one wicked stepmother
2. two wicked stepsisters
3. one invitation to a Royal Ball
4. one fairy godmother
5. one mouse-drawn pumpkin
6. one white ball gown
7. one petite glass slipper
8. one handsome and charming prince
9. one fairy tale wedding
10. one happily ever after

Activity 74

Sense and Sensibility

Think of a concrete object—a swimming pool, a gravel driveway, a forest, a tuba—or something more abstract like an emotion. Describe how it might taste, feel, look, smell and sound.
How does it make you feel?

Concrete

My leopard gecko is soft and bumpy and cool to the touch. He is bright like a smile, except when he is shedding. Then he is a ghostly gray shadow. My gecko smells like clean sheets that have been hanging outside on the line in a strong April breeze. He sounds like a cricket's worst nightmare, silent and deadly. My gecko tastes like a tiny desert cave, sandy and dark and secret. My gecko makes me feel like hiding in a closet with a sweater and a snack and a book about fire-breathing dragons.

Abstract

Anger is black: a runaway train hurtling out of control through the night. Anger tastes like bile and smells like burning wood. The sound of anger is an exploding bomb and people screaming. Anger is scalding, like boiling oil or freezing cold like nitrogen. Anger feels like the sulphur end of a blown-out match. It feels like walking barefoot through broken glass.

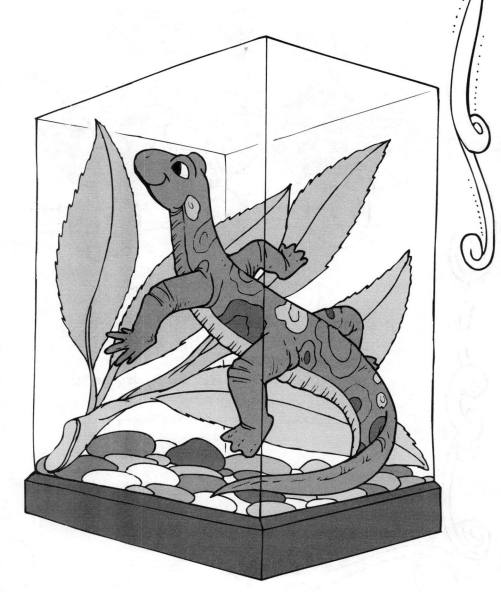

Activity 75

Silly Similes

A simile makes a comparison between two things using the words **like** or **as**.

As: honest **as** the day is long
     hungry **as** a horse
     sly **as** a fox
     nutty **as** a fruitcake
     smart **as** a whip
Like: **like** flies to butter
     like salt on an open wound
     like two peas in a pod
     like a bull in a china shop
     done **like** dinner

Write some silly similes by making outrageous or extravagant comparisons.

As

Wild *as* a five-foot flag in a hurricane, the coat whipped up around my face and threatened to lift me right off the ground.

Like

Like a mad hatter he was! Galloping down the street, snorting and thrashing and knocking people hither and thither *like a bull let loose in the streets of Pamplona.*

As and Like

Her nose was as shiny as a peeled onion, her eyes like two black olives. Her skin was as sallow as candle wax and the two or three teeth that remained in her mouth were like stumps in a stagnant swamp. She was as short as daybreak, and her hair hung around her ankles like coiled rope. Yet, she had a way about her that made me feel like a pauper in the presence of royalty.

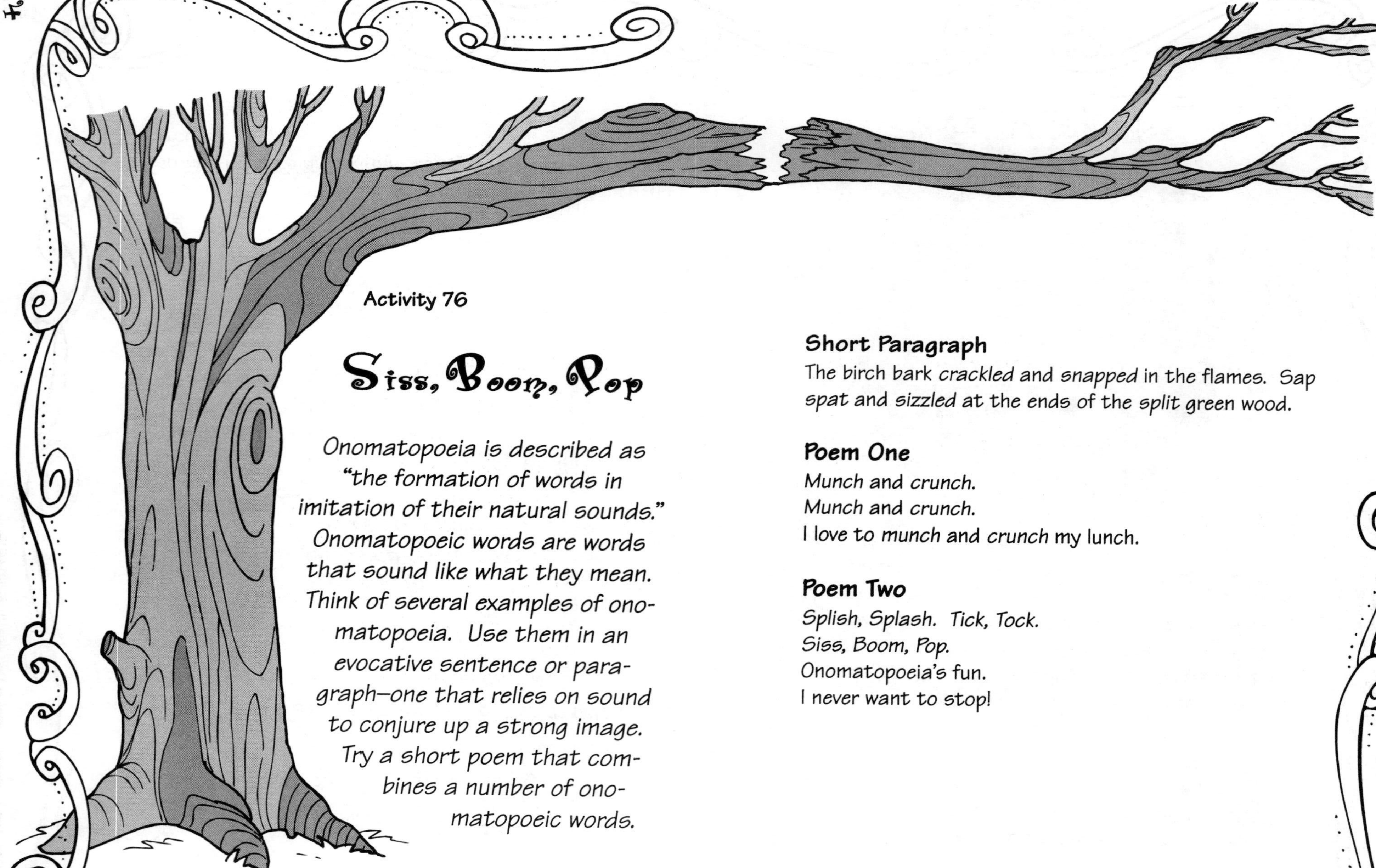

Activity 76

Siss, Boom, Pop

Onomatopoeia is described as "the formation of words in imitation of their natural sounds." Onomatopoeic words are words that sound like what they mean. Think of several examples of ono-matopoeia. Use them in an evocative sentence or para-graph—one that relies on sound to conjure up a strong image. Try a short poem that com-bines a number of ono-matopoeic words.

Short Paragraph

The birch bark crackled and snapped in the flames. Sap spat and sizzled at the ends of the split green wood.

Poem One

Munch and crunch.
Munch and crunch.
I love to munch and crunch my lunch.

Poem Two

Splish, Splash. Tick, Tock.
Siss, Boom, Pop.
Onomatopoeia's fun.
I never want to stop!

Activity 77

Sort It Out

1. Choose a theme: family, travel, movies, pets, school, music, elephants . . . . It can be anything that you know a little bit about.
2. Jot down about 10 words that are associated with your theme.
3. Write very short clues or definitions for each word.
4. Pick one of your words (five letters is a good length). This will be your **secret word**. (You must be able to make the word using one letter from each of five of your other words. These six words are now the only words in your game. The others can be discarded.
5. Draw a blank for each letter in your first word.
6. Circle the blank that is the letter clue for your secret word.
7. Beside your string of blanks write the letters of the word in mixed-up order.
8. Write the clue beside the scrambled letters.
9. Do the same for each of the remaining four words. For your secret word, all the blanks will be circled. There will be no scrambled letters and no clue.
10. Give your puzzle to a friend and see if he or she can solve it. Don't give any extra clues—and keep the clue to the secret word hidden—unless your friend gets really stuck.

1. _ⓗ_ _ _ _ _ _ _ _   racaehrsct   people in the story
   h–characters
2. _ⓐ_ _ _   eagps   usually numbered
   a–pages
3. _ⓞ_ _ _   ocrev   soft or hard
   o–cover
4. _ _ _ⓞ_   tsryo   plot line
   r–story
5. _ _ _ _ _ _ _ⓣ_ _   tlriltsorua   creates the artwork
   t–illustrator
6. _ _ _ _ⓤ_ _ _   ctruespi   drawings, paintings
   u–pictures

Secret Word

7. ⓄⓄⓄⓄⓄⓄ   (torhua)   (does the writing)
   (a-u-t-h-o-r)

Discarded Words and Definitions

title: what the book is called
contents: list of what is in the book
chapters: major divisions in the book
publisher: responsible for production and sales

Activity 78

Spain's Reign

Assonance is "the repetitive use of like vowel sounds." Spain reigns with what is perhaps the best-known example of assonance: "The rain in Spain falls mainly on the plain." Think of at least 10 assonant words. Use four of them in a sentence. Then try a sentence using five or more. See if you can make a sentence that uses all of your assonant words.

Four Words
Tonight, the moon's light is quite bright.

Five Words
The moon's light is quite a bright sight tonight.

All Eleven Words
The sight tonight of a bright white kite at great height in the moon's slight light gave me quite a fright, all right.

Assonant Word List
1. bright
2. fright
3. height
4. kite
5. light
6. tonight
7. quite
8. right
9. sight
10. slight
11. white

Superheroes

Create your own superhero. Name him or her. Describe him or her. What are his or her super powers? What is his or her secret identity?

Captain Organization

By day she parades her home as a mildly effective housewife and mother, trying to make ends meet with a part-time writing career and hanging onto domestic order by the skin of her teeth. But at night, when her unsuspecting and ungrateful family is fast asleep, Tracey Schofield leaps out of bed, dashes into the linen cupboard and dons the many hats of Captain Organization: the world's greatest super-efficient hero. Able to wash an entire day's dishes in a single sink; prepare the next day's meals with nothing but leftovers; do a week's worth of laundry in only seven loads; vacuum a houseful of carpets without a beater bar; scour the iron from the toilets with a flimsy paint scraper, scrub the ceramic floors to a sparkling shine using only vinegar, water and a small hand sponge; balance the checkbook by the light of the moon and write another chapter of a best-selling novel on an old 486. Three cheers for Captain Organization, world's greatest super-efficient hero. We salute you, wherever—and whoever—you are.

Activity 80

Synonym* Scramble

Write a sentence. Choose (at least) two words from the sentence and make a list of as many synonyms as you can for each of them. Rewrite your original sentence several times using replacement words from your list of synonyms. Which sentence do you like best?

(If you are stuck, try using a thesaurus—a dictionary of synonyms and antonyms—to help you choose the words you will use in your sentence and/or the synonyms for each of your words. Understand that not all of the synonyms will necessarily work in the context of your sentence.)

Original Sentence

The *journey* to their new *home* seemed *endless*.

Replacement Words

journey	home	endless
trip	domicile	interminable
tour	residence	limitless
pilgrimage	dwelling place	boundless
excursion	abode	continuous

Possible New Sentences

The *trip* to their new *domicile* seemed *interminable*.
The *trip* to their new *residence* seemed *interminable*.
The *trip* to their new *dwelling place* seemed *interminable*.
The *trip* to their new *abode* seemed *interminable*.
The *trip* to their new *domicile* seemed *boundless*.
The *trip* to their new *residence* seemed *boundless*.
The *trip* to their new *dwelling place* seemed *boundless*.
The *trip* to their new *abode* seemed *boundless*.

*synonyms: words that have the same, or almost the same, meaning

TLC10240 Copyright © Teaching & Learning Company, Carthage, IL 62321-0010

Activity 80

𝒮ynonym 𝒮cramble *continued*

The *pilgrimage* to their new *domicile* seemed interminable.
The *pilgrimage* to their new *residence* seemed interminable.
The *pilgrimage* to their new *dwelling place* seemed interminable.
The *pilgrimage* to their new *abode* seemed interminable.
The *pilgrimage* to their new *domicile* seemed boundless.
The *pilgrimage* to their new *residence* seemed boundless.
The *pilgrimage* to their new *dwelling place* seemed boundless.
The *pilgrimage* to their new *abode* seemed boundless.

The *excursion* to their new *domicile* seemed interminable.
The *excursion* to their new *residence* seemed interminable.
The *excursion* to their new *dwelling place* seemed interminable.
The *excursion* to their new *abode* seemed interminable.
The *excursion* to their new *domicile* seemed boundless.
The *excursion* to their new *residence* seemed boundless.
The *excursion* to their new *dwelling place* seemed boundless.
The *excursion* to their new *abode* seemed boundless.

If we use some of the original wording . . .
The *journey* to their new *residence* seemed interminable.
The *pilgrimage* to their new *home* seemed endless.
The *trip* to their new *domicile* seemed interminable.
The *excursion* to their new *home* seemed boundless.

. . . The possibilities seem endless.
 . . . The number of combinations appears boundless.
  . . . This activity could be interminable!

There are so many ways to say the same thing. To find the wording that suits your personal style and particular subject perfectly, you just have to play around with synonyms.

Activity 81

Tabletop Trivia

Make up some trivia questions about your family, friends and relatives (or animals, fruits and vegetables, things you drive, movies, astronomy, computer games, junk food . . .). Ask your trivia questions at the dinner table in game show format. (Make it a rule that contestants have to "buzz in" before they answer!)

Tabletop Trivia Game: Schofield Family Version

1. He stepped on Eeyore's foot at Disney World. — Buzz: Papa
2. Nana would like a bigger one of these . . . — Buzz: kitchen
3. She once ate a whole box of chocolates in one go. — Buzz: Bun (our dog)
4. None of our three work very well . . . — Buzz: garage doors
5. She killed her sister with an exercise wheel. — Buzz: Hammy (our hamster)
6. Where we go every summer . . . — Buzz: Nova Scotia
7. He licks his eyeballs. — Buzz: Gex (our gecko)
8. She loves animals. — Buzz: Stephie
9. Elise is the name of Daddy's favorite . . . — Buzz: Lotus (our car)
10. What Anniken does when you pick her up . . . — Buzz: bite and scratch
11. Patrick's favorite Christmas present last year . . . — Buzz: an RC car
12. Darth Maul is Matthew's favorite character in . . . — Buzz: Star Wars: Episode I
13. Mommy's favorite restaurant meal . . . — Buzz: fish and chips

Tabletop Trivia Game: Animal Version

1. Largest land mammal . . . — Buzz: elephant
2. Gets hit by boat propellers a lot . . . — Buzz: manatee
3. Bamboo is the favorite food of . . . — Buzz: the giant panda
4. The koala is not really a . . . — Buzz: bear
5. Spiders have this many legs . . . — Buzz: eight
6. Its spit is deadly. — Buzz: komodo dragon
7. Provides us with milk and cheese . . . — Buzz: cow
8. Egg-laying mammal . . . — Buzz: duck-billed platypus
9. Extinct bird (was large and friendly) . . . — Buzz: dodo
10. A chicken lays . . . — Buzz: eggs
11. Fastest land animal over short distances . . . — Buzz: cheetah
12. Nocturnal animals hunt at . . . — Buzz: night
13. Large cat with stripes . . . — Buzz: tiger

Activity 82

Taboo-Boo

Think of a person, place or thing (pp/t) and 10 of the words that best describe it. Now write a description of the pp/t without mentioning it directly and without using any of your 10 taboo-boo words (or any part of any of these words). Do not hint with rhyming words or "it sounds like." Read your description to a friend and see if he or she can guess the identity of your pp/t.

pp/t: computer
Taboo-Boo Words

1. monitor
2. keyboard
3. mouse
4. disk
5. drive

6. bytes
7. RAM (Random Access Memory)
8. internet
9. e-mail
10. typing

This is something that I use for word processing. It is a machine that I plug into the wall. I have a 486 although now you can use one with a Pentium processor that is much faster. I use a screen to see what I am doing and a printer to show me what I have done. I can connect this machine to my telephone line to get information from around the world.

pp/t: spoon
Taboo-Boo Words

1. eat
2. stir
3. scoop
4. cereal
5. bowl

6. knife
7. fork
8. cutlery
9. utensil
10. silverware

This is something that I use when I am having my breakfast. I hold it in my hand. It's what goes into my mouth when I am eating my bran flakes. I can also use it to remove a tea bag from my mug or to make my hot chocolate swirl around in my cup. You use one of these in baking to make "tea-" and "table-" size measurements.

Activity 83

Take It from Me

*What is the best advice anyone has ever given you?
What is the worst?*

Best

My daughter's neurologist gave me the most sage advice I have ever received. She told me not to push Stephanie with too many therapies when she was a baby and that the best thing I could do for my special little girl was to "just love her."

Worst

My cousin: "Try the cabbage soup diet. It really works." It worked pretty well for me. I slurped liquid vegetables for a week and actually *gained* weight.

Activity 84

Tear Jerkers

What makes you cry?

I cry a lot at movies. In fact, I cry at almost every movie I see. Sometimes I cry so loudly in the theater that the people I am with are embarrassed and threaten to leave. At some movies, I cry right from the beginning to the end. When this happens, I usually end up with a migraine headache that lasts for several days. If I even suspect that a movie is going to make me cry this much, I often decide not to see it just for health reasons. I am especially vulnerable to movies that involve long, drawn out good-byes, particularly if it revolves around someone's brave death, or a parent's death, or a child's death, or a pet's death or a wild animal's death . . . .

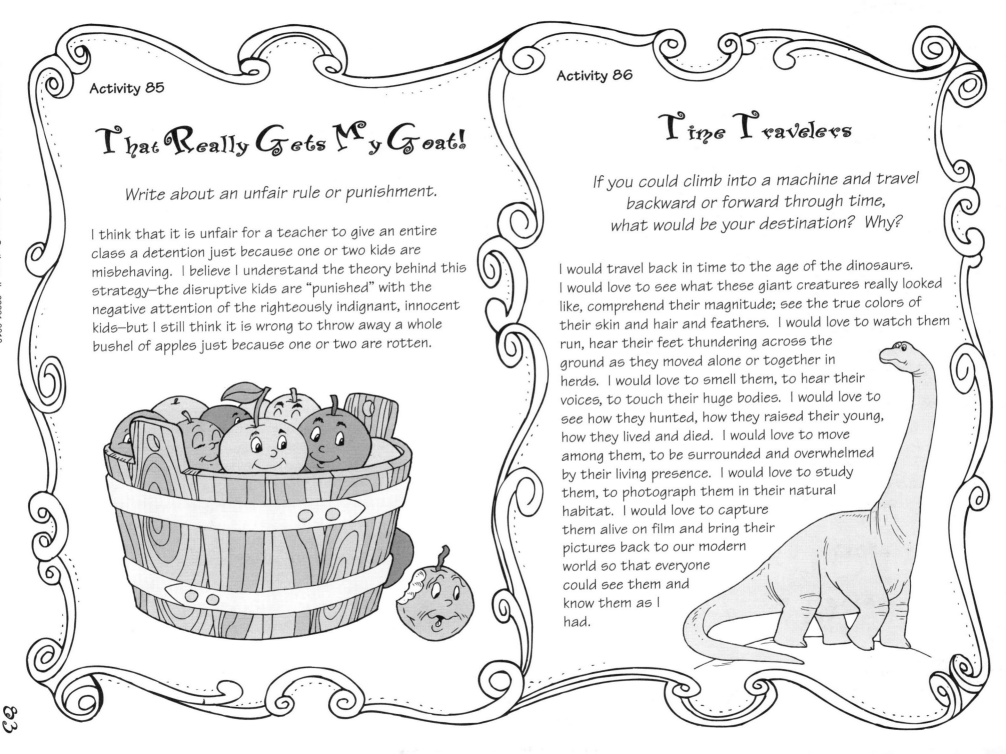

That Really Gets My Goat!

Write about an unfair rule or punishment.

I think that it is unfair for a teacher to give an entire class a detention just because one or two kids are misbehaving. I believe I understand the theory behind this strategy—the disruptive kids are "punished" with the negative attention of the righteously indignant, innocent kids—but I still think it is wrong to throw away a whole bushel of apples just because one or two are rotten.

Time Travelers

If you could climb into a machine and travel backward or forward through time, what would be your destination? Why?

I would travel back in time to the age of the dinosaurs. I would love to see what these giant creatures really looked like, comprehend their magnitude; see the true colors of their skin and hair and feathers. I would love to watch them run, hear their feet thundering across the ground as they moved alone or together in herds. I would love to smell them, to hear their voices, to touch their huge bodies. I would love to see how they hunted, how they raised their young, how they lived and died. I would love to move among them, to be surrounded and overwhelmed by their living presence. I would love to study them, to photograph them in their natural habitat. I would love to capture them alive on film and bring their pictures back to our modern world so that everyone could see them and know them as I had.

Activity 87

The Sky's the Limit

Describe your "dream" career.

My dream career would be working in the wilds of Africa, photographing and studying lions and giraffes and chee-tahs, and writing about my adventures and discoveries in articles published by *National Geographic* magazine.

Activity 88

These Are a Few of My Favorite Things

Make a list of your very favorite things.
Use single words, short phrases and/or sentences.
Try to write in paragraph or poetic form.

I love my kids. The way they smell, the way they sound when they are very much in love with me, the way they look when they are sleeping. I love my parents. The way they care about me, the way they worry about me, the way they never forget my birthday. I love my husband. The way he works hard to make sure we have a nice home and food on the table, the way he puts up with my eccentricities. I love my country home. The woods, the fields, the river, the birds. And I love the pictures I have taken to remind me of the things that I love: my kids, my parents, my husband, my home. These are a few of my favorite things.

Thematic Definitions

Think of a theme: music, literature, food, drink, furniture, cities, animals, jewelry, famous people, history, teachers at your school . . . . Write down at least 10 things that relate to your theme. For each of these, write a short definition or cryptic clue. See if a friend can use your definitions and clues to figure out your list words and decipher your theme.

Theme: Chocolate Bars

Thematic Definitions

1. A drinking establishment on the red planet. *Mars Bar™*
2. Our home galaxy. *Milky Way™*
3. Piles, heaps. *Mounds™*
4. Clever people. *Smarties™*
5. The head guy; paradoxically, the husband of Mrs. Small. *Mr. Big™*
6. Trio that adhered to the motto, "All for one and one for all!" *Three Musketeers™*
7. Compassion/Concern for a cow's liquid product. *Caramilk™*
8. Shot from a bow; Robin Hood's weapon. *Aero™*
9. Feline pair; baby and adult. *Kit Kat™*
10. Small laughs, usually behind someone's back. *Snickers™*
11. "Be _ _ _ _t and between." *Twix™*
12. Greasy pointer digit. *Butter Finger™*

Activity 90

Think Again

Think of a far-out use for an ordinary, everyday object.

This might look like an ordinary plastic place mat, but it's actually a polyurethane flying food carpet—perfect for safe and speedy "breakfast in bed" delivery. Simply place the food items and necessary utensils on the mat and say the magic words—*Abra ca dabra! Ala ca dead! Take my mother breakfast in bed!*—and your food carpet will be up and flying. When your grateful mother has finished her meal, two hand claps and the words *Place mat, return!* will bring the mat (complete with dirty dishes and food scraps) winging back to the kitchen for quick and easy cleaning.

Activity 91

Trading Places

If you could trade places with anyone in the world, who would it be? Why?

This is a tough one. I wouldn't really *want* to trade places with anybody. Any gains to be made by taking up residence in another body would be offset by the sacrifices I would have to make to leave my own. However, if I absolutely *had* to trade places with somebody, I guess I would choose Julia Roberts. She's wealthy, she's beautiful, she's incredibly popular, she appears to be happy and well adjusted and she gets to act for a living! How perfect does that sound?

Activity 92

Travel Teasers

Write a short "teaser" brochure that will make someone want to go to the destination of your choice: Hawaii, space, back in time to caveman days.

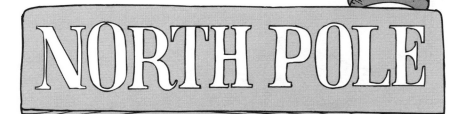

Come to the North Pole: Land of Ice, Snow . . . and Santa Claus!

Come to the North Pole, a Christmas winter wonderland where you will:

- Visit Saint Nick's workshop
- Sit down for gingerbread cookies and hot chocolate with Mrs. Claus
- Meet Donner, Dasher, Prancer, Vixen, Comet, Cupid, Dancer, Blitzen and all the other reindeer

It's not all white! There is so much to do and see at the North Pole. Grab a stick and play an afternoon pick-up game of hockey with old Kris Kringle himself. Browse the world's largest toy shop, and place your custom Christmas order with one of Santa's "elves behind the shelves." Take in a furry flying demonstration. Enjoy a hot turkey dinner and the spectacle of the Aurora Borealis from a cozy table at the Northern Lights Cafe.

At night, sleep in the cool comfort of the exclusive North Pole Inn, where every night is Christmas Eve and every morning is Christmas Day. Hang your stocking on the door before bed and wake up to presents! Join your friends for an early morning dip in the pool at the Polar Club. Waddle down for a festive "black tie" breakfast in the Penguin Palace. Then treat yourself to a breathtaking aerial sleigh ride high above town courtesy of Rudolph and his friends.

The fun never ends at the North Pole. We are open for Christmas getaways 363 days a year (closed for Christmas, December 24-25). Why not visit us today and see why so many people call the North Pole their favorite holiday destination? Ask your travel agent about sleighfare and accommodation packages that start as low as $1599 per person, per week, all-inclusive (gifts, too!).

The North Pole
Filling your days, and your stockings,
with Christmas fun all year long.

Activity 93

Triplets

Look out the window and/or around the room and write down the names of three objects that you see. Use these three words together in a single sentence. Use your triplets in two more sentences.

Triplets
- Telephone
- Snow
- Carpet

Sentence 1

I ran for the *telephone*, my boots trailing footprints of *snow* across the *carpet*.

Sentence 2

I sat on the *carpet*, staring absently at the *snow* falling outside my window and not really hearing my mother's voice on the *telephone*.

Sentence 3

The cellular *telephone* slipped out of my hand and disappeared beneath the thick, white *carpet* of *snow* lying in the driveway.

Activity 94

Utopia

Describe your perfect day, dinner, date, class trip, family holiday . . . .

My Perfect Pet

My perfect pet would not shed. It would not need brushing or bathing. It would not make me sneeze. My perfect pet would eat leftovers, instead of pet chow, so it would be very inexpensive to feed. My perfect pet could be left alone when I had to go out or slipped into my purse if I wanted to take it with me. It would be small when it was convenient, but pretty big the rest of the time. My perfect pet would not bark or meow. It would not chew furniture. It would not leave muddy footprints on the floor. My perfect pet would never need to go to the bathroom.

It would not dribble or drool, and its breath would smell like peppermints or cotton candy. My perfect pet would sit on my lap when I needed cuddling and lie on a chair beside me when I wanted to be by myself. It would play when I wanted to play and sleep when I wanted to sleep. My perfect pet would always be happy to see me, but never sad to see me go. My perfect pet would talk to me when I wanted conversation, but stop if I felt the need for silence. My perfect pet would never argue with me. It would never misbehave or disobey me, and it would always do what I wanted to do. My perfect pet would never get sick, and it would not die until I did. My perfect pet would be my very best friend—my perfect friend.

89

Activity 95

What a Difference

If you could change one thing about your life, what would it be?

I would make my best friends move closer to me so that I could see them whenever I wanted to instead of just once or twice each year. I'm lonely here without them, but I don't want to move again. I like my new house and I like my property and I like my little country community. If my friends could buy houses here, where I live, that would be perfect.

Activity 96

When I Was Two

Imagine what life must have been like when you were two and shorter than your kitchen table!

When I was two, I couldn't reach the light switch so I was scared of the dark. The counter was a mountain that I couldn't quite climb and the refrigerator freezer was as far away as the North Pole. When I was two, I had to walk down the stairs one at a time, holding tight to the railing so that I wouldn't fall. Every trip to the basement was an adventure that set my heart to beating. When I was two, I liked to drink out of the dog's dish. I crawled around on my hands and knees and barked at the postman when he put our letters through the slot. When I was two, I got a candy cane from Santa whenever we went Christmas shopping at the mall and my Mom's hand was an anchor that kept me from get-ting swept away in a sea of legs.

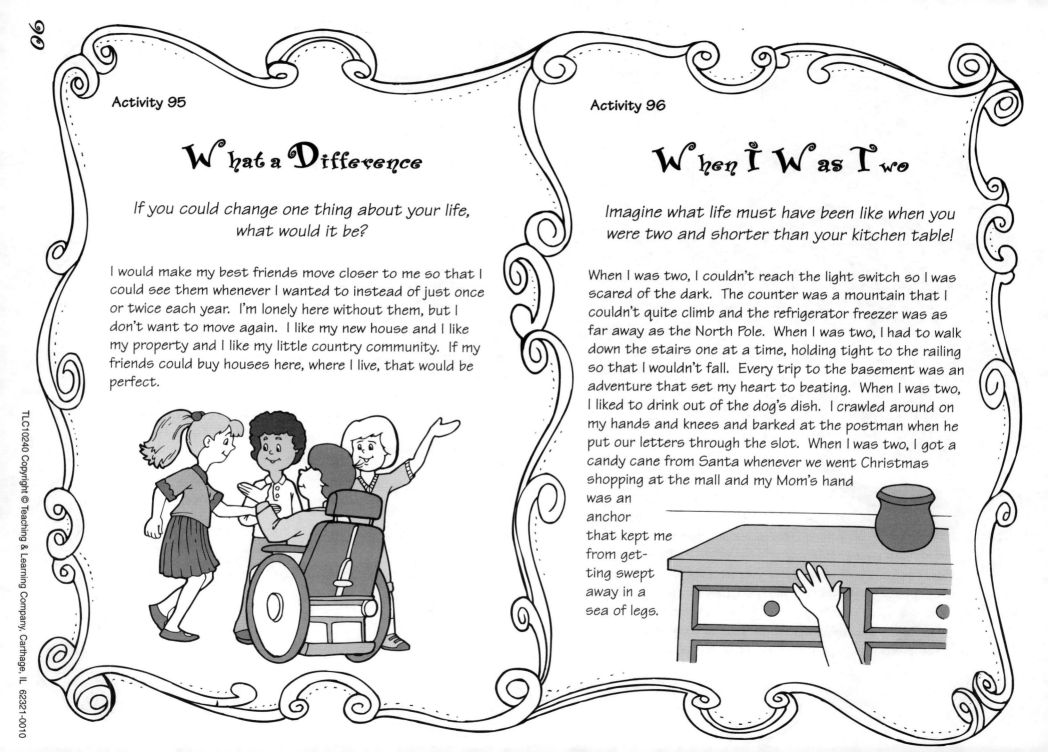

Activity 97

Wonderful Words

*Write down a word that you love
just because of the way it sounds.
What do you think the word means?
How does saying the word out loud make you feel?*

Polyglycerolpolyrincinoleate

This was an ingredient in one of my favorite childhood choco-late bars. It makes me feel like an old steam train starting to move away from the station platform. My wheels are struggling to turn to a whispery, 4/4 rhythm that empha-sizes the "polys" as we chug along, picking up speed.
Chug. Chug. Chug. Chug. Chug, chug.
Polyglycerol. Polyrincinoleate. Chug.
Polyglycerol. Polyrincinolee-chug-chug.
Polyglycerol. Polyrincinoleate.
Chug.
Polyglycerol.
Polyrincinolee-chug-
chug.

Sumptuous

I think this word means "delicious." (Actually, I just consulted my dictionary and it means: "involving or showing lavish expen-diture; hence, luxurious, magnificent.") It makes me feel all wiggly and warm, as if, really tired, I have just crawled into my bed and am worming my way down between my flannelette sheets, alternately stretching my body out and curling it into a ball.

Activity 98

Wordy Associations

Ask someone to say a word out loud. Write down everything that pops into your head when you think of this word. Use single words, short descriptive phrases and complete sentences. Use some or all of your favorite word associations in a paragraph or poem.

Night

- Dark, quiet, still
- The setting for night owls, wolf howls and skunk prowls
- The resting place of shadows
- A place where fear lurks in every fertile imagination
- A terrifying backdrop for howling wind, thunder and lightning, driving rain
- A time for resting and dreaming and growing
- Stars and moon, fireflies in June
- Like snowflakes on black construction paper

Night: Paragraph

At night the moon and the stars shine white like bright fingers of light poking through cut-outs in a black cloth or snowflakes settling in stark relief on a piece of black construction paper. In June, fireflies twinkle in the dark blanket of sky that sinks down and covers the Earth. With the children of the light tucked up in bed, the creatures of the night venture forth and lay claim to the darkness, shattering the quiet stillness with their restlessness: hooting owls, howling wolves, prowling skunks. At night, fear lurks in every fertile imagination, inserting itself into the cracks and crevices of the mind with tendrils of dreadful uncertainty. Shadows are living places. Wind and rain, thunder and lightning are palpable, living signals of danger and provide the perfect backdrop for irrational terror.

Wordy Associations continued

Night: Poem

The night is quiet, soft and still
A lone wolf howls upon the hill.
A striped skunk prowls my flowerbed
An owl hoots from overhead.

Nearby the fireflies shine and dim
Flashing on, then off again.
The moon and stars are glowing bright
I like snowflakes on a winter night.

Points of light on low and high
Piercing holes in blackened sky.
And yet their light cannot compete
Devoured by darkness; obsolete.

The night is blind in shades of gray
A shadow of its former day.
Familiar shapes are foreign things
Obscured by black that nighttime brings.

I breathe the silence, taste the night
Pull my covers 'round me tight.
I close my eyes, submit to sleep
And dream of day in slumber deep.

Activity 99

Write Me In!

If you could somehow transport yourself into an existing movie or book and assume the life and role of one of its main characters, which script or text would you choose and which leading character would you be? Why?

This is a difficult game to play since all movie and book characters are faced with difficulties and conflict—it is what makes their stories appealing and interesting and makes us relate to them sympathetically as fellow human beings. To make a choice, it is important to carefully evaluate the pros and cons of a character's situation and then choose one set of triumphs—and the trials and tribulations that go hand in hand with it—over another. For the good must, in the end, outweigh the bad.

This having been said, I think I might like to live the life of Harry Potter in the series of that name by J.K. Rowling. I would love to possess Harry's magical powers: to have the ability to wield a magic wand and to fly on a broomstick; to put spells and potions to good and helpful use; to establish true and lifelong friendships with people who think and feel and act as I do. Perhaps the exciting and noble outcome of Harry's life of wizardry would somewhat compensate him for the early loss of his parents and the years of neglect and abuse he suffered at the hands of his Uncle Vernon, Aunt Petunia and cousin Dudley Dursley.

Activity 100

Xcuses, Xcuses

Write some zany excuses that just might fly!

"Sorry I was late. I spilled a whole bag of sugar on the kitchen floor and my Mom made me clean it up with a toothbrush."

(This is a real excuse given to my grade 10 band teacher by one of my more creative—and chronically late—classmates!)

"I have to leave work on time tonight. I have a basement full of baby snapping turtles."

(Another real excuse! This time, my husband to his boss. We rescued 14 baby snappers from the road in front of our house and were waiting until Daddy got home to let them go.)

"I am just sick about missing my copy deadline. The book was finished, honestly it was, but I had a terrible accident and I lost it, every last page. You see, I stepped on a rotten board when I was crossing the suspension bridge on my way to Wanamaker's General Store to mail the manuscript and it was either hang on to a year's worth of work or hang on for dear life. I chose dear life. Dangling helplessly over the gorge, I could only watch as my precious package was swallowed by the seething rapids 1000 feet below my sneakers."

(Imaginary. There is no suspension bridge on the way to Wanamaker's General Store and Post Office. But there could be!)

Activity 101

You're Only Human

What do you love most about being human?

I love being able to express myself with words. I love to talk with my kids at night when they are tucked in bed and eager to share the news of their day. I love to talk on the phone to my Mom and Dad—just to hear their voices and know that they are still there. I love to talk to myself when I am lonely or bored or feeling creative in the shower. And I love to write. I love to write about the things that I see around me and the things that I feel inside. I love smothering a blank piece of paper with thoughts that only I could think. I love having the ability to make something beautiful or funny or moving or bizarre out of nothing but my mind and my fingers.

I love words: spoken words and written words. And words are truly human things.